DISCARD

# THE CHEAP
# HANDYMAN

# THE CHEAP HANDYMAN

## (AND DISASTROUS)
## TRUE TALES FROM A
## HOME IMPROVEMENT EXPERT
## GUY WHO SHOULD KNOW BETTER

**B.S. HARRIS**

TILLER PRESS

NEW YORK   LONDON   TORONTO   SYDNEY   NEW DELHI

TILLER PRESS

An Imprint of Simon & Schuster, Inc.
1230 Avenue of the Americas
New York, NY 10020

Copyright © 2021 by Brian S. Harris

First Tiller Press trade paperback edition May 2021

TILLER PRESS and colophon are trademarks of Simon & Schuster, Inc.

For information about special discounts for bulk purchases,
please contact Simon & Schuster Special Sales at 1-866-506-1949
or business@simonandschuster.com.

The Simon & Schuster Speakers Bureau can bring authors to your
live event. For more information or to book an event, contact the
Simon & Schuster Speakers Bureau at 1-866-248-3049 or visit
our website at www.simonspeakers.com.

Interior design by Laura Levatino

Manufactured in the United States of America

1  3  5  7  9  10  8  6  4  2

Library of Congress Control Number: 2020933906

ISBN 978-1-9821-5098-3
ISBN 978-1-9821-5099-0 (ebook)

Thanks to my kids, Scott and Leah, for inspiring me to write this book, and to my wife, Maureen, for enduring these escapades with me.

# CONTENTS

Contents

Contents

I finished writing *The Cheap Handyman* just before COVID-19 swept the globe, with all its serious and far-reaching impacts. Publication was delayed as we locked down, uncertain of what the world would bring, and I found myself feeling—like so many others—that I'd been chained to my home.

My wife wasted no time finding projects for me. Her philosophy was that too much idle time was not good for the soul. No sooner had I finished processing the fact that toilet paper and hand soap were now impossible-to-find commodities than I was handed a folded piece of paper. It was a bit yellowed on the edges, which told me she'd been saving it for a while. The honey-do list was longer than it should have been, and what better time to slap it on me than now, when I was in a saddened state and feeling powerless.

These past months have been an unexpectedly perfect time to get my hands dirty working on faulty appliances, doors that won't close properly, or stairs that creak too much—problems that I've ignored for far too long. After several weeks of hard labor, pretty much everything in the house was in good order. The stove was no longer on life-support, the downstairs light switch didn't give you a jolt anymore when you touched it, and the upstairs shower was free of the incessant, head-pounding drip. The only reprieve I was awarded was not having to paint the entire downstairs of the house. It was a crying shame that the paint stores were closed.

Perhaps unsurprisingly, I was not alone in my urge to dive in on a home-improvement project. Whether out of desperation, boredom, or a desire to feel some sense of control in the world around us, many people attempted DIY projects for the first time. If that's you, welcome to Team Handyman! I hope you know that you are not alone as you delve into uncharted waters. To go where you have not gone before is still good for your soul (and your pocketbook). There is always a great deal of personal satisfaction in completing a job successfully, but it is important to realize that you may be less than a hero from time to time, as not all jobs go as planned. An occasional jolt to the ego makes us better people. Failure is a good learning tool for future endeavors. I should know!

I hope that my experiences will give you the confidence to step out of you comfort zone, take on a new challenge, fail well and often, and fight through any issues that might present themselves.

Most of all, in an age where DIY projects are more challenging than ever, I hope that handymen and handywomen find in these pages the encouragement they need to get the job done.

Go for it, and good luck!

—Brian

"If it ain't broke, you're not trying."

—RedGreen

# THE CHEAP HANDYMAN

I remember the first time I realized I was a homeowner. My wife and I had just bought a beautiful cedar home, two bedrooms, two bathrooms, big backyard—it was the home we'd always dreamed of raising a family in. Not one month into home ownership, the furnace broke. No longer could I call the landlord—this one was up to us! From that moment on, as any homeowner can tell you, the to-do list was constant. As were the bills.

Now, anyone who knows me can tell you that I've always been a bit cheap. I suppose I come by it honestly: mine was an average, hardworking family—my parents taught me the value of money, and I was fortunate enough to earn a degree. Still, ask my wife and she'll loudly recount tale after tale of my miserly ways. I'm confident that I will never live down the time our family flew standby to Ireland, or the time I gifted my friend two tickets to see Elton John, only to get a real earful from him night-of when security wouldn't let him in—turns out the "deal" I fell for was a scam.

If there was a way to save a buck, I took it, and this is doubly true of home repairs. If hiring a contractor isn't highway robbery, I don't know what is! Lucky me, I'd always loved fixing things. Since I was a young boy I've just had to know how and why things ticked, and I spent hours tearing apart kitchen appliances and other gadgets, trying to repair them myself. It was just in my blood. I even had my own toolbox that contained a hammer, a screwdriver, a pair of pliers, and duct tape, of course.

I love spending time in hardware stores, both big and small, and I never miss an opportunity to drop into my local store. Whenever I'm within a couple miles of it, my car seems to just gravitate in that direction. I'll roam around the store for hours, more excited than a kid in a candy shop. There are so many cool tools and not enough time to try them all out. I even worked part-time in a hardware store for a while and was delighted when I could show people the different kinds of tools out there and what they could be used for. I could share my assumed and perceived limitless knowledge.

Every task I took on, big or small, was a challenge to me. I would sometimes have a mental tug-of-war going on in my head when I looked at the scope of a job. Would I be able to pull it off or should I throw in the towel? I often broke into a sweat thinking about what could go wrong, but invariably I brushed that thought aside and forged on. By and large, the projects went well. Upgrading to LED lights, winterizing the house, patching up a wall or two, fixing a leaky toilet—all easy enough. But every once in a while, I'd get it in my head to do something above my pay grade. *Electrical wiring? Sure! Why not? I mean, how different can the switch box for the pool be from a toaster?*

Now before you laugh, be honest: Have you ever felt the urge to take on a do-it-yourself project when deep down in-

Introduction

side you have serious doubts about what you might be getting yourself into? Have you ever said, "Hang on, I can totally do that myself!" even as you frantically google instructions? Have you ever shrugged off a well-intentioned hardware store employee and bought whatever you happened to have in your hand at the time rather than admit you forgot to measure before leaving home?

The lure of all that cold, hard cash you can save by doing it yourself has put many handymen and handywomen in over their heads. Before you know it, what started out as an innocuous weekend DIY project is a costly disaster. Some of my own mishaps have cost me very little, while some have cost me a great deal. Most of these experiences, however, have come at a greater cost than money itself: my pride.

My family and friends have enjoyed countless belly laughs at my failed escapades. And can I blame them? If I saw a man go ass over teakettle into a pool holding a chain saw, I'd laugh, too! Over the years, I've learned to laugh along with them, and ultimately it was those moments of sitting around the kitchen table reminiscing with my wife and kids, having a good laugh and seeing the smiles on their faces as they recalled my blunders, that inspired me to write this book.

The thing is, we all have a little cheap handyman or -woman in us, whether we choose to admit it or not. And while humorous stories can't fix a broken shower door or change your oil, they have a different kind of magic: they can repair the woes of the soul.

Best of all, as the adage goes, talk is cheap!

*Episode 1*

**W**hen you're a homeowner, there's always something that needs fixing. If it isn't the plumbing, it's rooms that need to be repainted, or replacing stucco that falls off the ceiling every time someone slams the door, or a washing machine that works only when it feels like it, and so on. Most days, it seems like there's always some problem or another to resolve. This day, the problem was the siding of my beautiful two-story, 2,500-square-foot, eighty-year-old cedar house—with the key word being *cedar*. It looked great until it was beaten up by the sun and wind. Its present fault lines and bare spots told me it was time for a face-lift.

It was a huge job to stain this monster, and not one I was eager to undertake, so I did what any prudent individual would have done and got a few estimates. But after I received the third quote, which was more than twice as much as the ones before it, I asked my wife to get the paddles ready for the "big one" I could feel coming on! I would have been ashamed to put to pen such outrageous numbers. I'd have to do the deed myself! *Besides*, I thought, *it couldn't be that bad*. I already had the extension ladder, so I'd just need twenty gallons of stain, five cheap brushes, one can of paint thinner to clean the brushes, a bag of rags, four drop cloths, two hooks to hang the cans from the ladder, and a bottle each of Tylenol and fast-acting pain-relief cream (in preparation for the punishment my body was about to endure), and I would be ready to go. Nothing a few days and some elbow grease couldn't accomplish.

I never considered myself a pro, but I did know enough not to stain a house on a windy day—which would be the equivalent of a child pissing into the wind. I also knew that, for the same reason, I couldn't use a sprayer. I was in for seven long days of brush and bucket work. I waited as patiently as I could for the right day to arrive. But after biding my time for a few weeks, the clear, calm day I needed never came. With my to-do list growing by the day, I couldn't wait any longer, so I was eventually forced to take my chances and begin with a slight hint of a breeze in the air.

With the ladder in place against the side of the house, I confirmed that all the necessary materials for the job were close at hand. As I began to climb up the two-story flight, I heard a creaking noise. At first, I thought it was the ladder but soon realized that it was my knees. It seemed to take forever to climb to the top. Looking down I felt like I was high enough to go skydiving. Then something dripped from my nose. I was relieved that it wasn't blood—just buckets of sweat pouring from my forehead. I carefully hooked my can to the step of the ladder and set to work. With the second dip of the brush the can tilted sideways, and I watched helplessly as the handle of the can broke off. It dropped like a rock, bounced a few times across the lawn, spurting stain in all directions until it found its final resting place against my neighbor's wrought iron fence. I was down the ladder faster than a fireman, grabbed a rag, and started frantically wiping the stain from his fence. I looked around for witnesses. None, thank goodness. No one would be the wiser. I'd deal with my brown grass at a later time.

I opened the second can, checked its handle carefully, gave it a good yank, and ascended the ladder. I worked meticulously, watching every movement of the brush. About an hour into the job it was time for a break. Back on the ground I admired my handiwork: I'd only done a small amount so far, and already the house looked new. Then something caught my eye. A closer inspection stopped me dead in my tracks. It looked like a flock of low-flying pigeons had machine-gunned their droppings all over my neighbor's backyard. Every inch of his in-ground pool, the patio furniture, cement, and landscaping was splattered with a brown film. There were even clumps of stain dripping off the statues he had beside his pool. Here I was being so careful not to put too much stain on the brush as I lifted it out of the can so as not to risk the stain flying all over the place. I also made the brushstrokes slow and smooth to keep all the stain on the brush and not somewhere else. The white rag in my hand was even stain-free! I was quite proud of myself for thinking ahead and keeping things well under control to avoid any problems, so how the hell did the stain end up next door? Who would have ever thought that stain would drift so far with such a little breeze—amazing!

I couldn't face the man. I was terrified! He was one of those neighbors who took such extreme pride in his backyard that his lawn was basically a putting green, which made this situation even worse. They don't call it *stain* for nothing—this was going to take professionals to clean up. It wasn't long before he stormed over, red-faced, and gave me an earful. I had to take it like a man! I nodded when he told me how we would proceed from here. I felt like a child being scolded for misbehaving.

It took about a week for the hired crew to clean up the mess I had made of my neighbor's yard while I focused on staining the other side of my house. I could just see the cash register smoking as each day went by. It was the longest week I could remember! They did a bang-up job on my dime. A lesson learned for sure.

**Estimated cost of job: $700**

**Actual cost of job: $1,800**

*Episode 2*

That huge, destructive branch had been driving me crazy for years. The lowest offshoot of a very old oak tree hung down in the middle of the driveway like the arm of the grim reaper. My wife's little Honda glided right under it, but it scraped the roof of my Ford pickup on every arrival, reminding me that I really, *really* needed to do something about that. Each time I heard it screeching on my roof, I strangled the steering wheel. I could only imagine how much paint had been ripped off the top of the truck. I didn't even have the courage to look. As much as I loved trees, that branch had to go.

A neighbor across the street was getting their tree taken down. It was impressive to see the big truck with the lift and box on it, high up in the sky. Dressed in the usual orange reflective jacket and wearing a hard hat, the guy was slicing and dicing the branches with his chain saw. They were dropping like flies. I stood by the supervisor on the ground and watched the show for a few minutes and then popped the question. He looked across the street at my branch and, without skipping a beat, quoted me a price. His response took my breath away, so I'd do it myself. I mean, how hard could it really be?

I gathered up my own chain saw, ladder, goggles, and work gloves and asked a buddy to come over to assist me. I didn't have a fancy orange jacket like the other guy, so I put on my old, beat-up, torn lumberjack's jacket and baseball hat. My wife was not home, so I didn't have to worry about her car; in order to keep my truck out of harm's way, I moved it from my driveway over to my neighbor's, about twenty feet away. I fired up the chain saw, and with my friend holding the ladder steady, I ascended. The chain saw made short work of the branch: within seconds it was plummeting straight down to the ground. I watched as it landed right on its end, recoil like a giant spring, and vault gracefully through the air, landing squarely on the hood of my truck parked innocently next door. It was as practiced a move as you'd see in a Cirque du Soleil performance.

The size and depth of the crease in the hood was daunting. Bad enough to see this affliction in my pride and joy, but I had just gotten her back from the body shop, where they had repainted the hood due to numerous tiny dents from walnuts dropped on it by squirrels. I always kept my vehicles in tip-top shape—each was always washed, waxed, and dent and rust free. The interior was so clean that you could eat off the floor. I was grief-stricken. I slowly came down the ladder in a depressed state. I nearly tripped over my buddy who was rolling on the ground in hysteria. I stood over him with the chain saw still running and did think for a moment of committing a criminal act.

## The Cheap Handyman

With great hesitation and embarrassment, the next day I limped back to the body shop. I was red in the face as I told him what happened. Being the professional he was, he tried to keep a straight face as he said he hoped to do as beautiful a paint job as before. I knew I was definitely the jackass of the month in his mind. I told him to paint the roof while he was at it—might as well line his pockets with more hundred-dollar bills.

**Estimated cost of job:** $0

**Actual cost of job:** $1,350

*Episode 3*

RADIO SILENCE

We used to have a gold 1998 Honda Accord SE sedan. It was the car that I drove for years, and I really liked it. I was used to my 2012 fully loaded Ford pickup, but this baby had all the bells and whistles of a new car: power everything, leather seats, even a sunroof. Best of all, it had a great stereo. I would crank up my country tunes and sing right along with them at the top of my lungs. Everything was great until I noticed one day that the radio had started cutting in and out. There was nothing more frustrating than singing along with your favorite song and then having the radio go silent on you. Maybe it was just me, but I felt a little self-conscious singing by myself. It made me realize that I couldn't carry a tune in a basket. It was imperative that I get the radio checked out.

I made an appointment with a car stereo shop in town to have them investigate the problem. It was a cool place. They specialized in installing new stereo systems and repairing radios. They had on display all kinds of setups ranging from inexpensive ones to others that would flatten out your wallet. The sound from these high-priced systems was just unbelievable. They made you feel as if you were in a recording studio.

**The Cheap Handyman**

As much as I'd love to have had the money for a better system, I was just in to have my radio situation diagnosed.

It only took the technician a few seconds to determine the problem. There was, without a doubt, a loose wire in the back of the unit. Years of the car pounding the pavement and hitting potholes had loosened the wire. If it was reattached properly so that the connection didn't wobble, the radio would perform perfectly. He said that even though it was an old radio, it was well worth fixing: Honda products lasted forever.

The only problem was getting at the unit. It was a nice display, but it was built right into the dash. The dash was attractive, with the bottom of it curving inward to add more styling. The main access to the back of the radio was behind the curved part of the dash. Three sections of the dash, starting from the left side of the steering wheel and moving to the right, would have to be disassembled just to get to the radio. At that point, all one had to do was slide under the dash, spot the loose wire, and fix it. The technician said it was a labor-intensive job and costly if they did it. He suggested I do it myself. Just take your time and keep your wits about you and everything should be fine. I was up for the challenge.

I moved the driver's seat back as far as it would go and tilted the steering wheel all the way up. I noticed there were a lot of screws to be taken out and how small they were. Starting on the first section I unscrewed each one slowly and dropped it into a drinking glass, for safekeeping. With all twelve screws out, I proceeded to pull off that section of the dash. It came out about an inch and then got stuck on the plastic casing around the steering wheel. No matter how much I twisted and yanked, that damn piece would not come free. I then spent another fifteen minutes removing the steering wheel casing so that I could continue. Section by section, I moved along until I had the three sections off and safely stored in the back seat of the car. I was now two hours into the job, had scraped every knuckle, and used my entire vocabulary of swear words. On the bright side, to my surprise and delight I didn't lose even one screw!

Taking a deep breath, I looked down at the radio that had caused me so much aggravation already. *Let's do this thing.*

Sliding under the dash was a feat in itself. It was a tight fit. I really had to suck in my gut to clear the bottom of it. On my back, inch by inch, I squeezed myself inward, until my noggin was looking directly up at the back of the radio. By this point I was deeply concerned about how I was going to get out. I guessed if worst came to worst, I could scream until I got out. I guessed if worst came to worst, I could scream until my wife or some passerby heard me. They could grab my legs and haul me out. There were wires coming in and out of the radio from all directions. It was impossible to know what wire was attached to what. It was so cramped under there that I couldn't even hold a flashlight in my hand in order to suss things out. I had been smart enough to bring a pen light as well, which I wedged between my teeth. Before I had started my descent under the dash, I had turned the car key to the right one notch in order for the radio to play. It was cutting out as I started grabbing one wire at a time and jiggling it.

Nothing happened with the sound until I touched this one red wire. It came right off in my hand and the music stopped. I was delighted. This was the culprit. All I had do was hit the little red plastic button, at the back of the radio that opened the hole into which the wire fit, slide in the wire, and then let go of the button and the connection would be solid. I'd be back in business. With the wire in hand, I slowly approached the red button but was diverted from my mission when my elbow banged off something and I accidentally touched the red wire to a green wire near the back of the radio. There was a zap and then there was silence, total silence—not even any intermittent music now. The one small light under the dash was no longer on either. I knew I was in deep shit.

Have you ever noticed how when you're in a rush nothing works? Clambering frantically, as I was trying to get out from under the dash and assess the damage, it was as if my head had grown three sizes. I had to fight to free it from the cramped space. My arms seemed to snag on every piece of metal under there. By the time I finally got out, I was really wound up.

I sat in the driver's seat and took a good look at the situation. There were no function lights or gauges displaying anywhere, and the radio was dead. Everything was dead. In one fell swoop I had fried the radio and burnt out most, if not all, of the electronics in the dash. I turned off the car, dropped my head, and wished I had a hammer in my hand right now.

I made another appointment with the stereo shop and headed back. At least the power steering was still working. I don't know why, but I didn't dwell on it. I would have popped multiple tendons in my arms if I had to manually steer that car over to the shop. The technician was quite attentive when I told him what happened. He said I'd have to leave the car with him, as it was often a long and tedious process to track down electrical problems. He said not to sit by the phone. It reminded me of sitting in hospital waiting rooms, waiting for test results. His words were ringing in my ears: "Take your time and keep your wits about you."

It was two days before I heard back from the technician. He said that they first checked out the fuses controlling the lights in the dash. Most of them were blown. Even after re-placing them, the dash was still as black as night. They next tested the switch, which controlled all illumination in the dash, and found it not working. In went a new one and voila, everything lit up like a Christmas tree. After all that, though, and as good as the technician was, he could not find a pulse in the radio. It had to be replaced. That's what happens when you get your wires crossed!

**Estimated cost of job:** $0

**Actual cost of job:** $320

*Episode 4*

## THE GUY WHO KICKED THE HORNET'S NEST

**T**he entrance to our attic crawl space was very small and tight. It was a challenge to fit into on a good day, but because of the high ceilings I'd had to make my own seven-foot ladder out of some two-by-fours just in order to get close to the crazy place. When not in use, I kept the ladder in the attic itself, on the floor. It took up a lot of space, so it was a logical place to store it. When I needed it, I stood on a step stool so I could reach the attic door, and I stretched as far as I could and pulled the ladder out. The only downside was that the ladder was incredibly heavy. Hauling it down was a hernia in the making for sure, but the procedure worked. I hated going up there and only did so when absolutely necessary, but this was one of those times. I was tired of tripping over the old books, fans, extra paintings, and other assorted, abandoned household items scattered all over the floors. Out of sight, out of mind was my philosophy, so rather than donate perfectly good things, I squeezed my reluctant body through the hole and into the abyss.

On the side of the wall I had installed one of those white-domed tap lights. Call me crazy, but I always felt there was some monster lurking in the corner waiting to attack me. I turned the light on and immediately heard a buzzing sound. I thought at first it was the light. I tapped it off, thinking it would confirm my suspicions. But the buzzing continued. Puzzled, I tapped it on and off a couple more times, but no dice. I'd just have to deal with the noise. I made a 180-degree turn looking for a spot to place the items and found myself staring nose to nose with a wasp nest the size of a basketball. I'd know that gray crepe paper piñata anywhere! There must have been thousands of them! I dropped a load right on the spot. This nest was massive, and the only thing keeping the wasps and me apart was a thin, plastic vapor barrier. Wasps hated light. They immediately got their knickers in a knot and now they had me in their sights. I was out of there and down the ladder like nobody's business. Something had to be done immediately as it would only be a short matter of time before they broke through the vapor barrier.

I made some desperate calls to the numerous exterminators I had tracked down, but the quotes seemed out of this world. I believe deep down that these guys really didn't want to come out—not that I can blame them. Going into an attic with a hive of paranoid wasps was like taking a knife to a gun fight in a dark alley.

The experts strongly suggested I watch the instructional videos online and that I could take care of this problem myself. I plunked my butt in front of my laptop and soaked up as much information as I could on how to get rid of them. As most of the videos recommended, I ran out and bought a special, potent liquid wasp killer (a machine that was similar to a large weed sprayer), a hose for the machine, and a long, three-foot-slender clear plastic wand about one half inch in diameter with a control lever on it. To be on the safe side I also bought a hazmat suit, protective plastic gloves, and a disposable respirator. I felt like I was auditioning for the next *Ghostbusters* movie, but at least I'd be prepared.

The video said the process was pretty straightforward. Fill the container with the liquid, make sure the top was screwed back on tightly, push one end of the hose onto the protruding stem of the container with the other end securely fastened to the end of the wand. Quietly and preferably with only a flashlight in hand so as not to upset the stinging machines, I would sneak up on the nest. With the free end of the plastic wand, I would poke a hole through the vapor barrier and continue through until the wand penetrated the nest itself. Spray copious amounts of the liquid into the structure and get the hell out of there. If all went to plan, those little buggers should have seen their last flight within a day, drop to the floor in a motionless state, and be ready for sweeping up and bagging for the next garbage pickup. A screwdriver would suffice to chip apart the nest itself for removal.

Drumming up the courage, I crawled on my gut to within about four feet of the nest, and then with my arm outstretched, I penetrated it and pushed the control lever. Nothing happened! I pushed it again and again and still no liquid came out. I dropped another load on the spot. The wasps were now officially pissed off and close to breaking through where I had made the hole. I had only seconds. I did a quick backward shuffle toward the exit, accidentally kicking the end of the ladder in my haste, sending it crashing down to the floor. Now in full panic mode I squeezed backward out of the attic, swung down with one arm like a deranged monkey, praying as I let go that I'd land without snapping an ankle. Thudding to the ground, I looked up to see if I was being followed . . . and noticed to my horror that I had not shut the attic door.

Yelling as I ran through the house, I grabbed my wife and kids and darted to the car, closing the windows and locking the doors, just in case some of those demons were in hot pursuit. The kids were screaming. My wife shook her head and looked at me in disgust. A look I'd seen many times before.

From the car I called the exterminator again. He was silent for a moment after I told him my story, and then he stated that not many people could have royally screwed this up but that he and his crew would come out the next day. He said to stay in a hotel that night and perhaps a second night as it sometimes took a few days for all the wasps to die.

When I got the all-clear call from the wasp boys, I was then firmly instructed by my family to go into the place alone, scope things out, and make absolutely sure that there wasn't even one wasp corpse in sight before they took a single step inside. I shamefully followed their orders. Like a SWAT team, I cleared all the rooms and gave them the go-ahead to come in.

**Estimated cost of job:** $90

**Actual cost of job:** $550

*Episode 5*

## IT'S A ROOF LIFE

It was time for me to reshingle the roof of our old cedar house. Those guaranteed-to-last-forty-years shingles were now on their last legs in less than twenty. They were dried out and curling up at the ends—the telltale sign that their life had expired. Anytime anyone within a twenty-yard radius sneezed, shingles would blow off. For the previous five years I had been hauling my derriere up onto the roof to replace shingles that had consistently blown off with just the slightest wind. Now, I wasn't going to be able to do the whole job myself—roof replacement is a monumental job—but it will, at this point, come as no surprise that I wanted to save money where I could, so I made the decision to do as much of the grunt work myself. I made a deal with the roofer that I'd strip the old shingles, leaving him only to put down the new ones. The price quoted was based on this. It was a relatively simple job, one that any handy person ought to be able to do without incident. I'd be working on a reasonably sloped roof with approximately one thousand square feet of surface area on each side. It was maximum a two-day job.

The weather for the next few days would be sunny and a comfortable temperature to work in, so I assembled the necessary items for the job, which included knee pads, good gripping shoes, work gloves, a hat, safety glasses, a crowbar, a ladder, sunscreen, and music in the background—country music always had a calming effect on me, particularly when things started to go sideways. I also needed *lots* of water. Sometimes the shingles got so hot from the sun that it made me feel like I was dropped in the middle of a desert. More often than not, you could see your butt smoking from sitting on them. At seven a.m., I ascended the ladder.

The shingles were so dilapidated that I could pull most of them off quite easily with my hands. Across the roof I went, row by row, starting at the apex and working my way left to right and back again. *This job might be easier and quicker than expected,* I thought. After about two hours I took a break to survey my work. The shingles were gone but not a single nail. They stuck up in rows that seemed to span for miles. It reminded me of some kind of torture machine where the poor bugger would be strapped to a bed of nails and left there in the blazing sun to fry. There must have been five hundred nails, and I'd only done a small portion of the roof.

Obviously, the nails had to go or there wouldn't be a way to attach the new shingles. So it made sense to me to pull them out or hammer them down, whichever worked the best. I grabbed my crowbar, went up to the first nail, and started to pry it out. The nail didn't budge an inch. I strained and passed lots of wind trying to get some movement, but there was none. As my backup plan, I grabbed The Beast, my favorite four-pound graphite hammer. It had gotten me out of many jams in the past. I recall using The Beast on numerous occasions to free up old, rusted pipes. A few good whacks loosened the joint but usually left a lot of collateral damage in the process. It was also helpful when I had to pound some of the pool heater parts back into shape that I accidentally stepped on. The Beast came through with flying colors, but unfortunately the parts were just too far gone.

I swung it as hard as I could and made solid contact with the head of the nail. The head bent a bit but nothing else happened. I began to panic slightly as I looked around at all the other nails. Mine was a very old home, and in those days they used solid-wood planks that were now pretty much petrified. The wood was so solid and tough that you could run a car into it full speed and never leave a scratch. That's what I was dealing with. I took a short break, rested up, and began pounding the crap out of random nails like I was trying to be the next whack-a-mole champion. Not one of them budged. I calmed myself, regained my composure, and decided to at least strip away the shingles. Perhaps overnight I'd think of something to deal with the stubborn nails.

Dusk was now just around the corner. I had removed the shingles from half of the roof, and I was beat. I called it a night, packed up, had my usual nightcap, and headed off to bed early. I was in a peaceful deep sleep until a loud crack of thunder jolted me awake. My eyes nearly popped out of my head as I realized that it was raining and half of the roof was exposed. I ran around like a madman looking for some tarps and something heavy to secure them. I finally found them wedged in the top corner of the shelving unit in my garage— *Why the hell had I put them there?!* I grabbed a few loose bricks we had lying around as well, put up the ladder, and headed up to the roof. Rain had been pounding down on the bare wood for nearly half an hour and it was drenched. Stumbling around like a drunk in the dark I finally had the tarps down and secured. Soaked to the bone and thoroughly pissed off, I entered the house ranting about how it wasn't supposed to rain that night. My wife, with all the commotion, had come down to see what was going on. Standing there in her bathrobe, she wasn't even listening to me. Instead she was staring up at the kitchen ceiling, watching water pour in through the main kitchen light fixture. Together we watched as some of the plaster around the light fell to the floor, spattering wet chunks across the linoleum. We were truly in a dark place.

I called the roofer the next morning and asked him if he and his crew could begin a day early. I said they could start by removing the rest of the shingles and somehow deal with all the nails. He was quick to reply and say that the original quote given was no longer valid and that the new one would be much higher. I agreed. He said to remove the tarps and let the wood dry in the sun for a few days to avoid the possibility of mold developing. He'd drop by in a couple of days and check things out before starting. When he did begin, I noticed his crew were all young and strong. It took them about three seconds to climb the ladder with a bag of shingles on each

24

**The Cheap Handyman**

shoulder. One of them had some strange-looking, awkward contraption in his hand. He approached the first nail and had it out in a flash. Then like a machine he popped out one nail after another and in less than an hour had every nail out of the half-stripped roof. The new roof was completed in record time, and in record time I was handed the bill. I wish I had become a roofer.

The kitchen itself was another matter. It had sustained water damage and would require a visit from a different kind of expert. My pocketbook and my nerves could not handle that shock right now, so I'd postpone it for a while.

**Estimated cost of job: $3,100**

**Actual cost of job: $6,300**

## Episode 6

## IT TURNED MY CRANK

**W**e like to open one of the upstairs windows in our bedroom so that we can hear the birds and other pleasant sounds as we drift off to sleep. Unfortunately, the cranking mechanism on the main window was stripped so that the window wouldn't open. The handle, when turned clockwise, should push the window out, but it just turned freely and did nothing. It would have to be fixed. I called a window company for an estimate. He told me that it was a special-order lever that would take about two weeks to arrive. On top of that it would cost a ridiculous amount for them to come out and install it. I wasn't about to wait or pay, so I'd tackle the problem myself, even though I'd never attempted something like this in the past.

I didn't know what particular mechanism was needed, so I'd have to take out the old one and hopefully find a label or something on it to help me identify what to order. Since nothing was working, I'd have to open the window manually. To avoid screwing things up I went online and reviewed a video on the best way to open a broken window and remove the defective parts. The video simply said to use your hand, gen-

The Cheap Handyman

tly push the window open, unlatch the control arm, and remove the easily visible screws holding the cranking system in place. As this window was about twenty years old, I knew there could be a battle.

Well, the window wouldn't open with the gentle gesture of a hand, so I became more aggressive. I pushed harder with my hand and then started banging it with my hand, still with no positive results. I was frustrated now. The only other option was to apply some of my hockey skills to achieve the necessary result. Like any good Canadian, I'd played a lot of hockey in my time, and on occasion one had to use a little muscle to take the guy with the puck out of the play. It seemed like a good idea to try that here. I let into the window with my left shoulder, and without warning it flew open, broke off the end of the control arm, and smacked hard against the siding. It hit so hard that the glass busted and trickled down into the gutter. Additionally, the frame of the window bent. I froze for a moment. I calmed myself and now focused on resolving this situation. I now had to not only replace the cranking mechanism, officially called the "casement window operator," but I'd also have to deal with the twisted window. It all started out so simple!

I started working on the cranking unit. There were four screws easily visible on the inside of the window. With my capacity for shallow thinking, I felt that removing them was probably all that was left to do now that I'd already busted off the control arm. The screws wouldn't budge, so I went to the garage and grabbed some lubricant. I sprayed it on the screws

27

and let it sit for a while. Pressing down hard with the screwdriver I started to undo the screws. I had to be careful and go slowly since I couldn't afford to strip them. I got three of the four screws out without too much effort but couldn't say the same for the last one. It was like trying to change a flat tire on a car. You get all the lugs off except the last one. I grunted and groaned and swore as I struggled with the last screw. After about fifteen minutes it finally started to loosen and come out. I was happy!

I thought removing the mechanism itself at this point would be a piece of cake, but not so. It was wedged in there like ten pounds of bologna in a five-pound bag. I tried to lift it up and down, tried to shift it from side to side, tried to twist it and was ready to start singing to it, but it never even moved an inch. Assuming it was just really stuck in there after twenty years, I retrieved my mini crowbar and tried to pry it loose. All I managed to do was bend it and take a chunk out of the white windowsill in the process, but it was still holding tough. For some reason I decided to squeeze my head out the window and look around. There, hidden under a white rubber flap, were four more screws. Why would anyone put screws there? Nonetheless I tackled these screws, and about half an hour later they were out.

The cranking system now slid out quite easily. It looked like an octopus with arms flying in all directions. With my magnifying glass in hand, I went up and down the shaft of the unit looking for anything to give me a clue as to its identity. I felt like I was looking for a secret hidden treasure map.

After meticulously examining every spot and scratch and dirt mark on the thing, I finally found four numbers and a name. That must be the answer to the puzzle! Sourcing replacement parts was pretty much impossible if you didn't have some numbers or letters or model of the item to refer to. I then went online and looked for manufacturers. It was like working a second career trying to find someone who still made this particular item. After several hours I struck gold, found a guy who stocked them, and ordered one. It would arrive in about a week.

The window itself was opened and looking lost. Once again, with a considerable struggle, I was able to free it. I took it to a window outlet. The salesman was very polite when he informed me that this style of window was no longer available as it was too old. He suggested that I replace it with as close a new model as possible or leave it with them and they'd pound the crap out of it and straighten it out as best they could. I chose the latter as a new nonmatching window would not fly with my wife. I put up a piece of clear plastic over the opening until the window was repaired and installed by the professionals. Every time I look up at the house now all I can see is this refurbished, still-bent-in-places repaired window. Even though it would do, the eyesore would remind me of my shortcomings for quite some time.

**Estimated cost of repair: $55**

**Actual cost of repair: $300**

*Episode 7*

Our family dog was a darling little Shih Tzu named Patches. We all loved him dearly. The kids had been begging for a dog for years, and we finally gave in with the condition that they would take him for walks, clean up after him, and so on. Of course, they didn't do any of that. I lost weight just chasing after him. He was a happy little guy without a mean bone in his body. He had really grown, particularly his legs. He went from basically having hard-to-see stubby legs to quite long legs for this breed of dog. With his larger size came a bit of confidence and attitude.

Patches was now just over three months old, and each day brought new adventures that we had to monitor. He had the highest IQ in the household, and we were always on our toes. He had his own crate and enjoyed spending a lot of time in there. When not in the crate he'd stroll around the house, just looking for something to get into. As with most puppies, he had an instinct for choosing items he knew he shouldn't touch. My favorite pair of slippers? Toast the day after he arrived. The second day at home I saw him dragging something around the house that looked like a piece of string. It wasn't string, it was my earbuds, but with one missing. He bit it right off and threw it around the place as a newfound toy. One of our barstools even had a chunk out of it now. The most comical thing was that he'd play like crazy and then just pass out. It was priceless to watch. We counted ourselves lucky that, by and large, he didn't destroy anything of great value; however, for some reason, he had a particular fascination with the kitchen and seemed to always gravitate there.

We'd just had our entire kitchen professionally renovated about a year before. New cupboards, floor, appliances, basically the whole nine yards. It was an expensive undertaking and we were very protective of it. Perhaps he was enticed by some smells in that area, but with his razor-sharp teeth and claws, we didn't want him running wild in there and destroying everything in sight. We needed to block him off from the kitchen, so I checked into the cost of some baby gates. The prices were pure gouging. I'd just use spare wood I had around the place and make my own gate.

I had some roughly two-inch-by-two-inch wood that I could use for the frame and some lattice strips from an old pool gate. The lattice wood was quite thin and not very strong, but we were only dealing with a puppy here. That was all the material I would need, along with some screws and wall mounts. This gate didn't have to look pretty, it just had to work. I cut it to approximately three feet high, with no door, and to avoid drilling holes I'd pressure mount it to the walls. I would use a contact-cement type of adhesive to glue one end of the mount to the gate. The other end of the mount had a screw adjustment on it which allowed for a tight fit against the wall. I headed to my workbench in the garage, and about an hour later it was completed. The framework was solid, and the lattice strips crisscrossed over the opening. He could see through them but that was all. It had about six different colors of wood in it and looked ugly. I guess I could have painted it, but who cares. With any luck our pup would grow out of this phase shortly anyway. I secured the gate in the opening and we did a few test runs with our puppy. We watched as he sniffed the new gate, poked and clawed at it periodically, and barked at it from time to time, but it looked like it would do the job. The kitchen was now totally off-limits. I was so pleased that I hadn't gone ahead and spent a lot of money. Sweet, sweet victory.

A few nights later we headed off to a party and felt comfortable leaving our little friend alone for a few hours. We had a good time, and as we came home and entered the house I could sense right away that something wasn't right. We quickly walked around the corner and saw our bright-eyed little guy on the kitchen floor chomping away on some wood. Clearly, he had been in there for quite some time, as the bottom corners of two of the cabinet doors had been chewed off and he was now feasting on a large splinter of wood he somehow stripped off a third door. My heart dropped. How was this even possible?! Had the gate fallen? No, the gate was still intact. Yet somehow little Patches was in there, terrorizing our kitchen.

After shedding some serious tears, my wife and I just had to know how he got in there, so we re-enacted the whole scenario of leaving for the party. We brought the little demon out of the kitchen, set up the gate again, and pretended to leave, then hid around the corner with our heads tilting toward the kitchen. He couldn't see us. The puppy went directly to the gate, planted his front paws in the holes of the lattice work, scooted up the gate like a professional rock climber, hopped onto a barstool sitting there and then onto the kitchen floor, all in less than a minute. I had to say we were impressed with his ingenuity and coordination, yet still very upset with him. For being on this planet for such a short period of time, this happy-go-lucky little charmer had already done so much damage.

There were reasons people paid the money for store-bought baby gates. The gates looked like jail cells, with narrow bars that ran from the top of the gate to the bottom. They were narrow enough so that no one, not even a puppy, could squeeze through, but more important no babe or beast could climb them. If I hadn't been so thrifty, our kitchen would not look the way it did now. To avoid even a hint of a further mishap, we headed off to the local pet store and walked out the proud owners of a sturdy, reliable gate. Installed in seconds, it was an ulcer saver.

Tracking down replacement doors for the kitchen was not the challenge I thought it was going to be. For once in my life, what I was looking for was not discontinued. The manufac-

B.S. Harris

turer said he'd order new doors and recommended that we pay the extra charge and have them installed properly. He could tell we couldn't handle any more stress.

**Estimated cost of gate:**  $0

**Actual cost of gate:**  $1,400

## Episode 8

## IT'S ALL ABOUT THE DETAILS

I'd had my sleek black sports car for about five years. It was still in mint condition and only had 22,000 miles on it. Even though I hadn't driven it that much, I'd had it long enough and was ready for a change. I decided to sell it. I thought I'd spruce it up a bit before putting it on the market by detailing it inside and out. There are many fine detailers out there, but I knew I could do just as good a job as them. The cash is always better in my pocket than theirs!

I spent a few good hours cleaning, shampooing, vacuuming, and detailing the inside until it was so clean that you could eat your lunch off the floor mats. It truly looked like a work of art! I then turned my attention to the exterior. I gave it a good wash and was ready to start the tedious job of waxing it. In the past I normally waxed my cars by hand, but as I wasn't as young as I used to be, I decided to invest in a polisher this time. With the "wax on, wax off" theory, I started at the back end of the car. The polisher was just humming, and before long I had completed the trunk. It was so shiny that I could clearly see my reflection in it. It doesn't get any better than that!

I then proceeded to the sides of the car, and even though it was more challenging with the door handles and mirrors, all was done within a reasonable length of time. I took a short break and strutted around the car admiring my handiwork. It really did make a difference, but it was starting to take its toll on my body. I was definitely getting tired.

The hood was the remaining part of this project—it was quite long and wide and would take a considerable time to wax. Nonetheless I started and sang some tunes, as I was a happy man working away. As was the case with the rest of the car, I worked slowly and carefully, making sure that not even one spot was missed. About forty-five minutes into it I was almost done with only one corner, maybe a six-inch square, to go. I fired up the polisher, and as I went to start it slipped out of my hand and landed on the unpolished corner of the hood. Instinctively I grabbed it, and in doing so I inadvertently pressed it down quite hard. I breathed a sigh of relief as I'd stopped it from hitting the ground and probably breaking. As I lifted it up to start again, there was a huge chunk of paint stuck to it. There was no paint left on the hood. It was gone right down to the metal. I nearly soiled myself right on the spot. How could something like this possibly happen? Didn't they make better paint than that? Paint should last for years! If it could stand up to all the weather conditions thrown at it and countless car washes, it sure as hell should be able to handle a polishing. I was outraged!

I obviously couldn't sell the car in this condition, so I first went to the dealership complaining that no original paint job should ever do this if the paint was correctly applied the first time. I insisted that the hood be repainted at no charge. It fell on deaf ears. They said it was not a paint defect, just a defective hand polisher operator. I was escorted off the property. I then bounced from one body shop to another looking for someone to show me some mercy. I even went to the backdoor, backyard, nonlicensed, nonexisting shops that no one would ever think of visiting in the shadows of the night. They must have all belonged to the same Friday night boys' poker club as each answer was the same. We can't just paint one corner of the hood as it won't match. We have our reputation to protect. The entire hood needs to be redone, and the cost for that is $500. I had no choice but to bite the bullet and ended up going to the body shop that laughed the least. When I did finally put it up for sale, I had to eat the $500. It wasn't very tasty!

**Estimated cost of job:** $5 0

**Actual cost of job:** $5 00

*Episode 9*

We had a relatively large wooden shed at the back of our property, old but sturdy. It seemed a waste of space to use it as storage for a lawn mower and other assorted garden stuff. It would make an excellent recreation room for the kids and me. Cleaning it out and sprucing it up, we could make it into a fun space.

Transforming it was an enjoyable and fairly easy job. I insulated it, replaced the floor, and put paneling on the walls. I then ran electrical wiring throughout the entire building for lighting and heat. I threw in a couch, tables, and a TV. It was now very cozy and ready to use.

The kids had a blast in it all winter. It was a huge success. Finally, a job I had not screwed up!

As the summer came around, the kids complained that it became very hot in the shed and really too hot to use. *No problem*, I thought, *I'll put in a window air conditioner*. I purchased a 12,000 BTU unit the next day. It was really much larger than I needed, but as it was (the only one) on sale for a great price, I'd make it work. The shed was about fifteen feet by twenty-five feet. I chose an end window into which I'd install the unit.

This way the air could blow through the entire length of the shed and provide the maximum cooling possible.

The unit was a heavy beast. I needed a wheelbarrow just to transport it from the car to the playhouse. I measured the width of the unit and compared it to the dimensions of the window opening. Just my luck, the air conditioner was two inches wider than the window. This is what happens when you go shopping unprepared. I should have measured the window opening before I left and avoided the extra work I now had to do. In my mind I thought it would fit, but I should have known after all these years not to rely on what my mind thinks. Not happy, I took the window out and restructured the side framework to accommodate the unit. The height was more than ample. I then built a solid platform that sloped slightly downward toward the outside of the building. It rested on the bottom of the windowsill and supported the unit, allowing the water to drain out of the shed. The unit was so heavy I had to volunteer two neighbors to lift and hold it in place while I attached the two metal support arms. Once done, the installed unit looked just as it should, slightly angled down with about 90 percent of it hanging on the outside of the shed. Success!

I plugged it in and fired it up. The vibration from the running unit made the whole shed shake. It reminded me of putting far too powerful an engine in a car. The unit itself shook like crazy, rattling around so violently in the window that it started to vibrate backward out of the frame. The two support arms buckled inward and the behemoth totally fell out.

On its way to the ground it took with it the entire window framework along with a four-foot strip of the shed wall. I had no idea that the wall was in such poor condition. It must have become very brittle from countless years of being tortured by the weather. I was surprised to see it fall apart from the vibration. When all was said and done, you could drive a small motorcycle through the opening. Once again, I stood before unexpected destruction, aghast and disgusted with myself.

I told the kids that, due to a structural problem, there would be a delay before we could install an air conditioner and that they'd just have to suck it up for a while. I returned the AC unit and explained that it did not work out. I'd return for another one once my new handyman job was completed.

**Estimated cost of job: $15 0**

**Actual cost of job: $35 0**

*Episode 10*

## ROPED IN

**M**y in-laws were coming over from Ireland for a visit, and I couldn't have been more excited. They didn't often have the opportunity to come over and see us, so this was a very special trip. I hadn't seen them in ten years. They were the nicest people you could meet. The only stumbling block for me was their accent. No matter how intently I listened to them, I could only understand a portion of what they said. For all I knew they could have said that I was the most pathetic, stupid loser that their daughter could have married, and I would have agreed with it. They were going to be here for two weeks, and we had all kinds of things planned, from road trips to a special request of my father-in-law.

One of the things on his bucket list was water-skiing. He had heard us talking about it for many years and how we used to go almost every weekend in the summer. He knew that I had grown up skiing, had introduced our kids to it, and, more important, had introduced his daughter to it. I think he wanted to be part of the family tradition. Back home it was not possible to ski. First off, you'd be skiing in the ocean which would be frigid and with waves the size of mountains. Second, if you fell, you may be gobbled up by a shark or some other nasty fish. He had never even been in a small boat like ours, let alone tried skiing—this was going to be fun. The kids were very good skiers, and my wife was way up there as well. The only problem we had with the Mrs. was that once up, she'd stay up and hog all the time. The only way to end her run was to either suck the gas tank dry or cut the engine and have her drop into the water.

We rented a cottage on a lake about an hour from our house, and the plan was to drive up there the following day. The day before they arrived, I did my usual inventory check of all the stuff that should be in the boat, including life jackets, paddles, fire extinguisher, skis, and so on. I made sure I had my special, homemade ski rope. I'd originally rigged it up a few years ago as a backup, but someone had stolen my last rope the summer before and I refused to pay the stop-your-heart price of $150 for a half-decent new one. I had some old rope lying around in the garage. It was showing its age but to my eyes it was still useable. I cut it to seventy-five feet, the same length as any store-bought rope (which included extra for at-taching the ski handle). I repurposed an old broom handle, cut it down to a tidy twelve inches, drilled a hole all the way through at each end, and fed through the rope. All in all, my homemade ski rope was identical to the store-bought ones, albeit much older and a lot cheaper.

It was going to be a great vacation. The warm weather we experience here was a treat rarely experienced in Ireland. You would seldom, if ever, sun bathe on a beach there, even in the summer. It just wasn't warm enough. And now, as an added bonus, we would get to water-ski while basking in the sun—it just didn't get any better than that.

We lucked out the day we strapped on the water skis. It was sunny and warm, with no wind and a lake as smooth as glass. A perfect, ideal day to have my father-in-law experience a most memorable event. He was the spotter in the boat at first and watched as the kids glided from side to side behind the boat. They had been skiing for a few years now, and, being in their early teens, they made it look so easy. It was now time for "the man" to give it a try. The beach where the skiers took off was relatively sandy. Christy, my father-in-law, waded in up to his waist and was assisted with sliding his feet into the skis. With a thumbs-up he sat back into the water, keeping his knees pulled tight to his chest like he was sitting in a chair, and lifted the tips of the skis. I didn't want to gun the acceleration the first time, as I was afraid it might rip his arms right out of the sockets. An experienced skier would have no problem with a fast takeoff, but I didn't want to risk it with a beginner.

With a moderate acceleration of the boat he immediately fell forward, headfirst, and was dragged about five feet under-water. The next few attempts were not pretty. There was an-other nose dive followed by a severe separation of the skis. If he hadn't let go of the rope, you would have heard bones crack-ing and tendons tearing, among other things. Suffice to say, it was a good thing he wasn't planning on having any more kids. With perseverance, at last he popped up on the skis. He never gave up! We were impressed. I towed him around the lake going only fast enough to keep him afloat so that he could get the feel of having these extensions on his feet. He must have been feeling quite comfortable on them as he motioned me to speed up. To my surprise, he left his comfort zone directly behind the boat and, leaning to one side, bounced his way over the wake and off to the side of the boat. All smiles, he repeated the exercise and was now on the other side of the boat. Before long, he was zigzagging from side to side like a pro.

I thought he must be pretty damn proud of himself, so I decided to swing back in front of the beach so his wife and the other spectators could see him in action, and he could show off a little if he wanted. As I was about thirty yards out from the beach, he leaned to the right, and just as he crossed over the wake the ski rope broke. Out of control, he started flailing his arms in the air, trying to keep his balance. At rocket speed, he approached the shore, skied right out of the water onto the shore, and kept sliding about thirty feet until he was stopped by a cottager's clothesline. He hit the line midriff high, did a quick complete flip, and landed hard on his back on the sand. His skis had left his feet as he impacted with the clothesline and just kept going. He reminded me of a wrestler getting body-slammed onto the hard mat before being counted out. Everyone on shore rushed over to make sure he still had a pulse. It was an ugly scene to witness from the boat. I quickly returned to shore and got the briefing. The paramedics were on their way. He was strongly encouraged not to move and just wait, which he did. I knelt down beside him. He remained

## The Cheap Handyman

dead still with only his eyes staring up to the sky and occasionally blinking. He couldn't even talk, but if he could, I'm sure he would have had a few choice words for me.

The paramedics arrived in quick order and immediately gave him oxygen by placing a mask over his nose. Within a few minutes some body parts started to twitch, and before long he was sitting up. Shortly afterward he was helped up to his feet. He had a huge red band across his stomach where the clothesline had left its autograph, but remarkably he was otherwise unscathed. He sat on the back bumper of the ambulance while they did a few tests.

He was not a young man anymore, and they insisted that he go to the hospital for further tests. We followed behind the ambulance. We just piled into the car still in our bathing suits. We were tense and hoped that his body didn't have any more meltdowns on the way to the hospital. While the tests were being done, my mother-in-law informed me that their benefits would have covered a hospital stay and surgery if necessary, but nothing else. I was looking forward to being presented with the bill for the paramedics' visit, the ambulance ride to the hospital, the X-rays, the ultrasound, and the pain medication, not to mention the realignment of his dentures.

**Estimated cost of job:** **$150**

**Actual cost of job:** **$850**

*Episode 11*

Our cedar house was quite old. In fact, very old. It was basically a cottage that had been added on to over the years. The fixtures and blinds hanging all over the place seemed even older. The vinyl blinds had become an off-white color and were patched up in numerous spots with clear Scotch tape. Some of the ends were curled up so far that you had to yank like hell to pull them up and down. The fixtures probably hadn't been sold in stores for fifty years. My wife had been after me for years to do something about these atrocities, but it hadn't been on the top of the list. It was there now. They were bringing the place down. While I didn't often see the point in spending good money on new items when the old items did the job, for once we were both in agreement that they had to go, and the sooner the better.

My wife loved shopping, and she found what she wanted in a store that was, of course, as far away as possible. For once, I didn't ask how much it would cost. But the charge for delivery was another matter, plus it would be a long wait for our order to arrive. I'd just borrow my friend's trailer and grab it myself. My buddy's trailer was a nice-looking, solid motorcy-

46

cle trailer. It was almost too good-looking to use, but nevertheless it would help me out greatly.

I felt confident that I had everything I needed for the trip: the trailer (of course), some tie-down straps, tarps, and rope, just in case. I also had a copy of the trailer ownership in case I was pulled over by the police. If they nabbed me for a burned-out taillight, they'd most certainly want to see the ownership. Trailers are very easy to steal if one has the mindset to do it. I thought it was best to be safe than sorry. I didn't hit the road until about four p.m., as I was finishing up some chores. It would be about a four-hour round trip on the highway, plus half an hour to load the items. Off I went.

I got there close to closing time to find only an elderly bean pole of a man waiting for me. Soaking wet he may have been ninety pounds. I asked him where everyone else was, as I was expecting some assistance in loading all the stuff, but he said they were all gone. I didn't have the heart to put this poor guy to work, and, besides, I didn't want anyone having a coronary while helping me, so I loaded everything myself. There were ten boxes in total, and they were, to my surprise, quite light. Part of me wondered if lightness meant cheapness. . . . I guess we'd find out soon enough. I guess the old guy felt kind of useless just watching, so he grabbed the tarps and tie-down straps and secured the load. He looked like he knew what he was doing, so there was no need to check his work. Locked and loaded, I was ready to shove off.

I was about an hour into the trip when a car came screaming up beside me. The window opened and a finger pointed back to the trailer. I looked in the rearview mirror and saw the tarp on the right side flapping wildly in the wind. I pulled onto the shoulder in a panic and got out. The tie-down strap had wiggled itself loose. When I lifted the tarp, I froze. Most of the boxes were no longer in the trailer. To be exact, eight of the ten were now strewn along the side of the road somewhere over the last one hundred miles. I was thankful that the back strap had not broken and dumped the load into the middle of the highway—someone could have been seriously injured— but I was really in a tough spot now. It was getting dark, and I knew nothing more could be done until morning. I'd have to retrace my steps from when I left the factory and scour the landscape in the hope of finding my stuff. That would be a tedious job.

I called my wife and told her not to keep the dinner warm for me. I was driving around in the wilderness, lost, pissed off, and not overly impressed with myself. I was in the middle of nowhere and wasn't familiar with the surrounding area. I kept driving until I saw a sign for a motel and took the cutoff. It was a very old, small, dodgy-looking town. Looking down the road I could see a pub, restaurant, church, and motel and not much else. I saw the vacancy sign blinking and pulled in. There was only one other car in the entire place. Never a good sign. Still, I was exhausted now and too tired to drive any farther, so I booked a room. I could only hope the sheets were newer than the hotel. I'd crash for the night, rest up, and retrace my footsteps in the morning. It would be a real blessing if I could recover my lost merchandise.

**The Cheap Handyman**

I slept like a log. When I awoke, I walked to the restaurant across the street. A good breakfast and lots of hot coffee would pump me up for the long day ahead. I was quite relaxed considering everything. I should have been tapping my foot on the floor and aggressively biting my fingernails after what I'd been through, but for some reason I wasn't. Maybe it was the calm before the storm. I just sat there and gazed out the window. I turned away and then immediately looked out again. Something wasn't right. I could see the number seven on the door of my room and my car parked in front of it. People were checking out and packing their suitcases into their cars. It wasn't until the guy parked next to me loaded his bags into his trunk and, comparing his trunk to mine, I made a mental note of how much more storage space he had that it hit me: I shouldn't be able to see my storage space at all. There was no trailer. Someone had stolen my buddy's beautiful motorcycle trailer, along with my newly purchased merchandise. I was in deep shit now! What made it even worse was that he'd given me his special trailer lock kit to use, which fastened to the hitch and trailer so that no one could steal it. I had been too lazy and tired to put it on. I marched right over to the hotel's office and spoke with the manager. He didn't even look up. He just pointed to the sign above him that said NOT RESPONSIBLE FOR MISSING OR STOLEN ITEMS. He then pointed down the street to the police station.

The police officer was very pleasant as he gave me the paperwork to fill out. He said things had just been booming lately with all the thefts of cars, trailers, and boats. He said there was pretty much a zero chance of recovering the trailer. By now it had been repainted and shipped somewhere far, far away. He asked why I hadn't put a trailer lock on it. I didn't answer. I left the station having totally wasted my time.

Trailer or no trailer, I still had to retrace my steps. I'd better get going.

I headed back to where this whole nightmare began, the factory. It made no sense to look for the packages from this side of the road as trying to look across the median and through traffic to the other side would be a waste of time. I raced back and prayed that no unmarked police car was lurking in a ditch some place with a radar gun. Back at the beginning and retracing my steps, I cranked my head to the right and scanned the countryside as I putted along the road. I was on a two-lane highway, which made it difficult to drive too slowly. Even though I was in the right lane, I did receive an assortment of middle fingers and horns blaring, but I stuck to my guns. Twenty minutes along I saw some debris resting against a chain-link fence. I rushed over and was delighted to see it was one of the boxes. I carried it to the car and looked inside. It was a matching pair of blinds and not a scratch on them. Thank god. Back on the highway I crept along, and a few miles down the road I spotted more refuge. This box had flown from the trailer and slammed into a big rock. It didn't look healthy at all. From the side of the road the box looked more oblong than square—not a good sign. I looked inside to see a gorgeous, expensive-looking chandelier busted into a hundred shimmering pieces. I traveled for hours, it

The Cheap Handyman

seemed, and never spotted even one more of the missing six boxes. When I saw the hotel cutoff sign, I knew my goose was cooked. Almost all of the newly purchased items were lost at sea. All that money wasted . . . not to mention having to face the wrath of god when I got home. I didn't even want to go there. But even worse than that, I didn't know how to tell my friend that he'd never see his trailer again. I thought I should probably just head off to some remote island.

**Estimated cost of trip: $5** 0

**Actual cost of trip: $3,5** 00

*Episode 12*

DON'T TRY THIS
AT HOME

Along one side of our backyard, screening our in-ground pool and the deck from nosy neighbors, ran an attractive board-on-board wooden fence, behind which were a number of beautiful trees that provided shade and ambience for the backyard, and one dead, ugly, rotting tree stuck right in the middle of the other ones. It wasn't that large—probably only about fifteen feet high—but it turned my crank every time I looked at it. It had to go.

As always, I called around for quotes, and, just as I feared, the quotes I received were criminal. I'd have to undertake the chore myself. I did have all the equipment needed, ranging from a chain saw, extension ladder, eye protection, work gloves, and hopefully the necessary skills to pull this off.

Having watched professionals do tree removals at neighbors' homes, I felt quite confident that I could take down this tree effortlessly. I strategically leaned the ladder against the back side of the tree so that I could reach around it and start carving off some of the unnecessary branches before starting in on the trunk itself. Once on the ladder I climbed to the

52

upper part of the tree, fired up the chain saw, and reached around to the side of the trunk to cut off the first branch. I had hardly started when I felt the ladder move. I froze! Should that happen? Without warning, the entire tree shifted, and I thought I was going to crap my pants. I turned off the chain saw and waited for the aftershock. Within seconds the whole tree, from the roots up, started to topple over. From my high perch, I wrapped my arms around the trunk as it timbered over, sliced through the wooden fence like a hot knife through butter, and landed in the pool. I could hear the pool liner ripping as I went underwater. I climbed out of the pool, wet chain saw still in hand, and looked at the destruction. The branches had ripped huge gouges in the liner and water was escaping at a rapid rate. My heart sank!

After a few moments of sympathy, my wife and kids, who were sunbathing poolside, broke into laughter. They had looked a little concerned when I first tackled the tree but soon dismissed it as just another chore I shouldn't be doing. No one died so they thought it was okay to say it was the funniest thing they'd ever seen. Their only regret was that they didn't have their cell phones with them. The pictures would have been priceless.

For the cost of a case of beer and some burgers on the barbecue, a few friends and I got the tree out of the pool and did temporary repairs to the fence. The pool was pretty much empty by now. I was mortified when I told them what had happened. As solid friends tend to do, they couldn't swallow

B.S. Harris

for the laughter. I reminded them that "what happens here stays here!" When they left, I looked at all the damage I had caused and just shook my head. I finished off the case of beer myself. Definitely the right thing to do before making the dreaded call.

**Estimated cost of job: $0**

**Actual cost of job: $3,800**

## *Episode 13*

IT'S JUST NUTS, I SAY

I always enjoy when fall comes around. Leaves start to change color and it signals that another summer is coming to an end. The fall, however, also has its challenges. We had in our backyard this beautiful old walnut tree. It was monstrous, and it engulfed a good portion of the yard. As well an attractive-looking tree, it was also a huge pain in the butt in that it was the local shopping mall for squirrels within a one-mile radius. They would be scurrying up and down it twenty-four seven.

That tree had become a bone of contention in the neighborhood, as there were always squirrels running around and doing substantial damage to people's homes and property. In the summer they'd dive from branch to branch, dropping walnuts everywhere, including on top of peoples' cars, trucks, boats, and anything else harmlessly minding its own business. No one appreciated the dents left behind. In the winter they'd dig their way into corners of garages looking for a warm retreat. On one occasion I saw them steal insulation from a homeowner's crawlspace to make their winter home as cozy as possible. It was my home! They chewed right through the plywood covering the crawlspace entrance and just helped themselves. I think everyone's personal favorite annoyance was having the buggers constantly darting across the street, stop in the middle, contemplate changing direction, and then do who knows what. For the driver it was a heart attack waiting to happen.

Every year neighbors *begged* me to cut down that tree. A couple of them even went as far as to get the phone numbers of companies that would pay dearly for a walnut tree. They made for great furniture, and these trees were becoming scarcer by the year. These companies would even come to your home with all their equipment, cut down the tree, and haul it away at no expense. Much as this appealed to me in some ways, I loved trees and would not part with this one: it was an old, endangered tree that made a beautiful addition to our backyard. I had to deal with my fair share of walnut bombing inconveniences, but I would rather spend the extra hour to rake up the hundred-plus walnuts that the squirrels had so thoughtfully scattered across my lawn than cut down such an old beauty.

I mowed the grass every Saturday, and on one morning in particular it would be no different, except for one thing. This year I was taking a shortcut. Not long before, I broke my ankle on a tennis court and was now in a walking cast. It was difficult enough just pushing the lawn mower with a bad foot let alone raking up walnuts to boot, so I chose not to rake the walnuts this year.

The lawn mower was an older, self-propelled monster that was heavy and unwieldy at the best of times. Still, I liked that it covered a wide area of the yard and that the blades made mincemeat of the grass. I figured its blades could easily handle the walnuts, so I fired up the machine and sorted out how I would cut this grass with all the obstacles in the way. I decided to have the grass shoot toward the outside perimeter of the lawn and then halfway through have the grass shoot inward toward the tree. I figured that in doing it this way, I was less likely to step on a walnut and snap my other ankle.

The plan was working fine for the first ten minutes. I was very careful going over the walnuts, as I didn't want them exiting the lawn mower in a careless fashion. I then came up to a clump of them sitting in front of me. I should have skirted around them, but out of laziness, I surged straight ahead. There was a rumbling in the blades, and then like a rocket being fired, a whole bunch of walnuts flew from the lawn mower and made direct contact with my neighbor's car, parked a short distance away in his driveway. The blast was so intense that it took out the rear back door window on the right side of the car and pitted both the front and back door. The car looked like it had been parked at the wrong end of a firing range. I stopped the lawn mower and just gazed. What a mess! It didn't take a body shop expert to know that two new doors and a window would be in order.

This neighbor was a decent guy. I was so relieved it was the neighbor who lived on the left side of me and not the guy on my right side whose house I plastered with stain. This fellow was up in years and laid-back. He looked at the damage, didn't get too mad, and told me what body shop would be doing the repairs. I tried to talk him into going to my body shop, as I was probably eligible for a loyalty discount by now, but he said no. He said he would show me the courtesy of letting me see the estimate, even though he was going to go ahead with it anyway, whether I liked it or not.

**Estimated cost of mowing grass:** $0

**Actual cost of mowing grass:** $1,900

*Episode 14*

IT "FLOORED" ME

Every time my wife and I sat down in our living room, we'd comment on how old the carpet looked and that we should do something about it. Tired of having the same conversation over and over again, I said let's do it now. As always, I did my research. It seemed that most people no longer put down carpet and instead replaced it with some kind of solid flooring. You could choose from various colors and thicknesses of laminate or hardwood or engineered hardwood or vinyl. It took hours of work and patience for us to travel from store to store checking out the products and getting quotes. About a tank of gas later, we had three quotes. Each one was within a few hundred dollars of the next, and all of them were out of this world. What amazed me the most was that the cost of installation was almost double the cost of the flooring itself. After some deliberation we decided on hardwood flooring, which seemed to be popular with many of the house contractors. It was substantially more expensive than the other choices available, but it looked great, and as we had decided to install it ourselves, we'd come out okay in the end. Despite my previous misadventures, my wife even agreed to this undertaking. The quotes for the installation had made her take a deep breath, too. We weren't going to pay those bandits what they wanted for installation. We'd show them. I'd do it myself along with the help of some of my hockey buddies.

We had the flooring delivered. They started unloading it on the street at the end of my driveway. I ran out and asked them to please put it in the garage as I was not getting any younger. They responded with a definite no, reciting that insurance wouldn't permit it. Even a cash bribe didn't help. They drove off leaving thirty heavy boxes in a heap on the road a good distance from my garage. The next morning, and after some begging, I was able to get a few of the participants to assist me in stacking them in the garage. Not really a good start to this project.

I had to do some basic manual labor before calling in the troops. I removed the baseboards securing the carpet to the perimeter. It was so old that it came off in pieces rather than in the originally cut strip. I'd now have to replace all the trim at the end. I started ripping up the old carpet, and as I did I was pepper-sprayed with fine dust particles. It was so old that it just crumbled as I touched it. I had hoped to just peel it back, roll it up, and be done with it. This clearly wasn't going to happen. I stopped production to buy a mask, work gloves, and knee pads. It was going to be a long, nasty job.

After half a day of grunting and swearing I had the loose carpet bagged. Left were hundreds of fragments cemented to the floor. Looking down I could see that my kneecaps were pointing outward instead of in front of me. I was already regretting taking on this project. I popped some pain pills, grabbed a paint scraper, and got back to it, wasting another half day scraping the remaining debris off the floor. I was tired, but I was done.

Remarkably, I was quite mobile when the crew arrived the next morning. I had coffee and donuts there for them. I didn't want anyone bailing on me. We were all keen to get started. None of us had ever laid this kind of flooring before. We were all relatively intelligent and didn't foresee any major problems. I had another buddy come over who was a self-proclaimed expert at laying floors. He said it was important that the first row be properly lined up, and then the rest would just fall into place. His services were only needed for a short period of time and then he was gone.

Each crew member had a job allocation. Two slugged in the boxes from the garage, one did the measuring, one the cutting, two the installation, and one the supervision (me). It was impressive how quickly the flooring went down. The only real delays were moving the furniture from one side of the room to the other, especially that honking heavy grand piano. Nonetheless the flooring was laid in its entirety and the furniture moved back to its rightful place, all within about eight hours.

The floor was absolutely to die for. I was profoundly grateful to the gang and bought pizza and beer for our celebratory congratulations of a job well done. After their departure I picked up some trim, cut it to size, and installed it. It was truly the crowning touch to making the floor look magnificent.

Over the next few months we entertained more than usual, as we wanted to show off our new floor. I even went as far as to offer my services should any of our friends decide to put down flooring. I was truly proud of this great achievement.

As the cold winter weather started rolling in, I was still pumped with our new floor. One night I was in bed and just staring up at the ceiling, still thinking that we had been very smart to install the flooring ourselves. My thoughts were interrupted by a faint sound. I held my breath so that I could hear more clearly. All of a sudden there was a cracking sound similar to the noise my knees make when I bend, twist, walk, and sleep. My wife jumped straight up, and within seconds we were both hightailing down the steps. What we saw was something you'd never dream of. Our beautiful new floor had started to buckle everywhere. It looked like a mini mountain range full of peaks and valleys spanning from wall to wall and corner to corner. There was even a wide-ranging collection of splinters that could easily stab someone. I was ready to heave as we navigated our way to the kitchen, where the whiskey was.

After downing my third drink, I pulled out my laptop and looked up hardwood installation. How could things have gone so wrong? Right there, staring me in the face, was the important message in bold print stating that a sufficient space must be left around the perimeter of the room to allow for expansion and contraction of the wood depending on the weather. I

## The Cheap Handyman

was smoking now! It's funny that my good buddy had forgotten to enlighten us on this small, insignificant point. It probably didn't help that we had high humidity in the summer. It brings with it excessive moisture that can cause the wood to swell and create pressure between the planks.

The next few days were quite painful as I had to reorder the same flooring and broke down in tears when I said yes to installation.

**Estimated cost of job:**  $2,000

**Actual cost of job:**  $6,800

## Episode 15

## NOW ISN'T THAT JUST

## FOB-ULOUS

**W**e had traded up from our '98 Honda for a newer car, which started by pushing a button. I thought this was downright magical. That key fob allowed me to do almost anything as long as I was within a reasonable distance from the vehicle, usually about ten to twenty feet or so away. Our previous cars had always been much older and pretty much on life support. None of them had even one bit of this technology.

Our new car had treated us well for the year or so we had it, but as always things started to fail. I noticed that my fob was only working about 50 percent of the time and just assumed I needed to change the battery. I went to my local electronics shop and bought a new battery. I was shocked at the cost, but I had no choice. I had to be able to start my car! The man at the register offered to install it for a flat fee; I said they should be ashamed to charge more than the cost of the battery for installation. Not acceptable to me! I'd install it myself.

I looked at the fob and figured out how to get it apart. It would require a very small screwdriver to undo the ridiculously tiny screw on the back of it in order to get at the battery. I had to dig out the special set of tools I used to repair my glasses, which I broke on a regular basis. The screwdriver in there would do the job.

The kitchen light was the brightest in the whole house, and even with that I could hardly see the screw, let alone undo it. I fumbled around in our junk drawer for a magnifying glass. I felt like a surgeon with all kinds of contraptions strapped to his head, about to undertake a complicated procedure. I very carefully removed the screw. Off popped the back and there, clearly exposed, was the battery. It was secured in a circular bracket with three tiny metal arms wrapped around it, all mounted on the motherboard. The arms couldn't have been more than a quarter inch long and even narrower than that. With a quick pry job, it was free. I noticed as I was taking it out that it wasn't fitting as snugly as I thought it should. There seemed to be a little movement, which I didn't think was right. *No problem*, I thought, *this is why they make needle-nose pliers.*

Delicately, I bent the metal arms to make for a tighter fit. I bent the first two just a hair and moved to the last arm. I bent it gently and as I pulled back the pliers, I saw that the metal arm had broken off and was stuck to the pliers. *Uh oh.* I wasn't that worried, as I'd just solder the arm back on. I had used my trusty old soldering iron in the past for similar types of intricate work, so I fetched it and heated it up. With one hand, holding the tiny piece of metal in the pliers, I positioned it at the break point. With the other hand I put the paste and solder on the joint to be soldered and grabbed the iron. It always fascinated me how the solder, when heated up, would flow around the joint like hot lava, then cool off and become solid as a rock, thus cementing the two parts together for the repair. I pulled back the iron and didn't move a muscle for a few minutes, then slowly removed the pliers. Everything looked good. I peeked through the magnifying glass for a closer look. It looked like a good solid connection. The solder had encompassed both loose parts and solidly joined them together. To be doubly sure, I tapped the repaired arm with my finger . . . and it immediately fell off. *Hmm . . . That shouldn't have happened! Maybe it needed more solder.* I tried the same procedure three more times with the same result. It was clear to me that from this angle the solder wasn't getting far enough into the joint.

The only option left was to pry out the motherboard and turn it sideways, which would allow me to shoot some solder into the back of the joint. Reinforcing both sides of the joint would hopefully provide me with a firmer connection overall. With my tiny screwdriver, I oh so carefully pried up the corner of the motherboard, but only enough to allow me to get my needle-nose pliers in there. The pliers slid in and as I started to lift the board, a small piece of the board and a couple small, shiny-looking metal saucers immediately broke off. I was really ticked off now. Fed up, I just pushed the board back into place, secured the battery with the two remaining arms, and shut and screwed the thing back together. I stomped outside, stood close to the car, hit the fob, and nothing bloody-well happened. Thinking that loose battery was still to blame, I took the thing apart again, got some quick-acting glue, and stuck the damn battery back into its bracket. I made sure the glue was dry and that the battery was going nowhere, assembled it again, and did the point-click thing. Nothing, not even a small flicker from one of the lights. My fob was dead! How could something so simple become so complicated? Since when did we need remotes to start our cars anyway?!

I jumped into my truck and headed to the dealership. There, I explained what had happened. He opened the fob and immediately said that me breaking the motherboard fried the whole thing. I could now use it as a paperweight. I asked him to grab me another fob and I'd be off. He said life wasn't going to be that kind to me. A new one, which had to be ordered and specially programmed for my car, would be a whopping $295. To think I could have had the electronic shop put in the new battery for $10.

**Estimated cost of job: $5.95**

**Actual cost of job: $295**

## IT'S JUST A-DOOR-ABLE

Our downstairs bathroom had two sliding shower doors that had to be removed in order for me to clean the bottom plastic track in which they slid. It was a basic fiberglass molded shower stall with no tub. The doors were about six feet high and stretched to about three inches from the floor. I had tried to clean the track and had removed some of the dirt, but it still looked like some unidentifiable fungus was lurking around. My plan was to take off the doors, unscrew the eight-inch track, soak it in some soap and water, and then scrub the hell out of it. In the past I had removed and fixed numerous closet doors similar to these. To take off the doors, all I had to do was lift up each until the wheels attached to the top of the glass were free of the top track, pull the door toward me, and slide the door down. It couldn't be a simpler process.

To be on the safe side I grabbed some work gloves so I'd have a good solid grip. These doors were well-made and heavy. I also put on my clunky work boots as I was going to be working from inside the stall and didn't want to be slipping around. I stepped in, grabbed the sides of the door about halfway down, and gave it a good lift up. The door rose and popped right out of its track. I pulled it toward me a bit and bingo, it was free. Very carefully I moved it around, took it out of the stall, and laid it against the wall. I followed the exact same procedure for the second door, but for some reason I could not lift it high enough to clear the track and slide it out. The door rose about one quarter inch and then hit the top of the metal framework. This was not right. I should have been able to lift the door at least an inch or so, in order for the wheels to clear the track. I tried again with a little more pizzazz and had the same result.

As with every jam I found myself in, I went online and checked out the videos. This was the first time they let me down. I watched five videos on how to take off these crazy doors, and each one said to just lift the door out of its track and it would then be free to move out of the way. None gave any suggestions on why one door would come out and not the other. I went back to the scene of the crime, this time with my flashlight. I stuck my head as far up the door as I could to look at the track. I could see the wheels in the track, but with very little clearance at the top. It would move a very small distance before it hit the top of the framework. Absolutely no way could that door be lifted high enough. On a closer inspection, I noticed that it was only one wheel that was getting stuck. The track was bent up for a stretch, restricting movement of the wheel. I grabbed a screwdriver, pliers, and a hammer and tried to push it down, but I was unsuccessful. It was quite possible that the track was defective from day one and that the installers just somehow forced the door onto the track and then left it that way. Unfortunately, that didn't hold water when it came to taking off the door. At this point I could think of only one way to remove the door. It was risky and something I really didn't want to attempt, but desperate times call for desperate measures, and I was desperate.

In two places, at the top of each glass door, were metal brackets. One end of each bracket had a metal wheel attached to it, which slid into the track. The other end of the bracket was affixed to the glass itself with three screws. On the defective part of the track I'd have to remove the screws and gently let the door slide out of the bracket. I thought it best to first lift out of the track the side that would come out and then work on the other side. The good side lifted out easily, and I rested it on the bottom plastic track. I started to slowly undo the first screw on the other bracket when, for no reason, that entire side of the door fell straight down out of the bracket. I was unprepared for this. I didn't even have a good grip on the door. The entire door then fell forward, banged off the toilet, cracked on impact, and landed on the floor. The noise of the crash could have awakened the dead. Once again, I was at a loss for words. I could see multiple large cracks spanning out in all directions from the initial point of impact. This door had seen its last day of service.

These doors were frameless and had beautiful hand-crafted designs on them, which resembled trees blowing in the wind. Sadly, there would be less blowing now. This poor fallen tree deserved better than such a senseless, uncalled-for

The Cheap Handyman

demise. I had a local bathroom expert try to track down the same door. If Lady Luck was with me, I'd only have to order one. Unfortunately, the manufacturer of these doors was no longer in business. I'd have to open my wallet wide to pay for two new doors.

**Estimated cost of repair:  $0**

**Actual cost of repair:  $1,100**

*Episode 17*

I was a motorcycle buff and owned a gorgeous-looking machine. This particular bike was a 1400cc Harley-Davidson. It was a touring bike, and with the power it provided I could go on long road trips and never get very tired. Previous bikes of mine had smaller engines and weren't really designed for long trips. On these types of bikes you get bounced and beaten up every second of the trip and are totally exhausted at the end of each day. I remember the first stop when I got home from these trips being the chiropractor. I was so proud of my Harley and always liked to show it off, except when it was grimy. You could have a dirty kitchen, a dirty garage, or a dirty car, but you could never have a dirty motorcycle—it was simply not acceptable. I could have it detailed at the bike shop down the road, but I preferred to do it myself and save a little cash in the process.

It was a nice day, not too hot and perfect to work on the bike. I moved my deluxe, hydraulic motorcycle lift into the shade and onto the most level part of the driveway. It was important that the wheels of the lift were as firmly planted on the ground as possible, as I didn't want it rocking back and forth as I was cleaning the bike. Slowly I drove the bike onto the lift and tied it down tightly with my four special ratcheting straps. Next, I carefully raised the lift to about waist height to make working on the bike easier. I opened my bag of assorted waxes, debuggers, washing products, chrome cleaners, tire cleaners, and everything else available to man. It was time to clean up this beauty.

I started polishing and buffing as my favorite tunes played in the background. I don't know what made me sense it but for some reason I felt like I was leaning over the bike more and more as I was cleaning it. I kept going though, until I heard a loud snap as one of the straps let go. Like a huge ship listing as it started to sink, my bike leaned away from me. Instinctively I grabbed the remaining straps, held on for dear life, and tried to slow down the descent. I knew this was going to be a do-or-die situation. The bike was so heavy that it was dragging my feet along the ground. I was on the losing team in a tug-of-war—I think I blew out a kidney fighting this losing battle, but in the end, I was pathetically and disgracefully hauled over the top of the bike, bumping and scraping both shins along the way. It was no fun being raked over foot pegs, exhaust pipes, and a gas tank. To no avail, the nine-hundred-pound machine tumbled off the lift and crashed unceremoniously to the ground in a puff of smoke. I stared in disbelief. I was relieved to see that my reproductive parts were still intact. I then looked down at my bleeding legs, which needed medical attention.

My buddies and I felt as if there had been a death in the

family as we looked at my crumpled bike lying motionless on the cement. Oil was seeping out all over the place. We all shed a few tears as we picked it up and surveyed the damage. No one said a word, but the silence spoke volumes. Humpty Dumpty could be put back together again, but it would take considerable work and expense.

Workers from the dealership rolled around the next day. I could see the sadness in their eyes as they pushed the bike onto the trailer. They lovingly wrapped blankets around the bike as they gently laid it on its side. It was an emotional experience, but not as emotional as it would be when I received the bill.

**Estimated cost of the work:** $0

**Actual cost of the work:** $1,500

*Episode 18*

## BATHROOM BEDLAM

You know, being retired isn't always all it's cracked up to be. Sure, all that vacation is nice at first, but once the honeymoon period wears off, it can get a little dull. Some pick up a new hobby or just sit around all day driving their wives crazy. I worked part-time at a retail store to pass the time. The store was one of those proverbial one-stop shops that sold electrical and plumbing products, tools, and other assorted home goods. I was retired from my main profession but my wife still worked and I needed something to get me out of the house from time to time. If I stayed at home all day, I'd start watching too much TV and would end up planting roots there. Additionally, it gave me some spending money, and some spice in life is a good thing!

This particular company had these humongous sales periodically, and even though all the employees dreaded working at these times almost the entire staff was recruited to show up. There must have been sixty staff on duty. I was about an hour into my shift when an emergency message was sent through each of our headsets. One of the two toilets in the men's restroom had stopped working for some reason. The manager had called some plumbers, but none would be available to come out until the following day. He couldn't wait that long. This was a staff restroom and with the number of men working that day, one stall simply would not suffice.

The manager was frantically looking for some solution. As he passed by my department, I could see the stress in his face. Feeling sorry for him I mentioned that I was a handyman and had fixed numerous toilets in the past at my home and would look at this defective one if he wished. I felt it was the right thing to do—share some of my talents with others. He was ecstatic and said to just grab whatever parts were needed to fix it.

I felt quite proud of myself as I marched into the bathroom. Toilets were usually a pretty straightforward fix. Most often the problem I'd experienced was a toilet than ran constantly. It usually needed a new flush valve or fill valve. If it still ran, then I'd replace the flapper as water may be seeping out of there. I could do something special for the boss and perhaps earn some points in the process. Examining the toilet, I could hear the water constantly running. I lifted off the top of the toilet tank and immediately spotted the problem. The fill value was no longer working properly, which meant the bowl could not fill up with water. It just kept running. I'd replace the entire float apparatus and we'd be good to go. There were lots of them in the plumbing section.

I scrounged up some tools and began working. It looked like this toilet had been there for centuries. The bowl and tank were mounted quite a bit lower than those of today, making it difficult to work on. Before crawling under it I turned the water shut-off valve and removed the remaining water in the tank. I then lay on my back and, like a mechanic squeezing under a low sports car, I slid under the tank. Man, was it tight! I could hardly squeeze my melon in there far enough to see what was going on. I started to manually unscrew the plastic nut that secured the end of the water line to the tank. I'd only turned it slightly when water gushed out and sprayed me in the face. I was so cramped that I couldn't even get a rag in there to wipe off my face, so like a dog I just shook my head from side to side. I then very carefully unscrewed the nut the rest the way, let if fall down harmlessly onto the floor, and pulled the line away from the tank. Decades of old rust, grime, slime, and other unidentifiable fungi fell directly onto my face, but I trudged on. I did notice a minuscule crack in the bottom of the tank right where the hole was but thought nothing of it as there was no evidence of water leaking in that area. One has to be very careful when working on old plumbing. All you have to do is look at it and it would start leaking.

I gently removed the inside parts of the tank, slowly slid in the replacement unit, and carefully directed the protruding extension into the hole at the bottom of the tank. Tilting my melon to the side I slid back under the tank. All that was left to do was line up the water line with the extension, simply put the plastic nut into position, and hand tighten it. This was all done in short order. I then slowly turned the water back on and tried out the new equipment. The toilet was now purring like a kitten. I hung around for a few minutes to make sure there were no leaks and then left. It was a job well done. All smiles, I told my boss that we're now back to 100 percent and returned to my post in the hardware department.

Shortly afterward, while helping a customer, I heard over my headset that there was massive flooding in the bathroom areas and not to go there unless you were wearing rubber boots. With the manager on my heels I ran to the men's restroom only to see the entire floor submerged. To make things worse the ladies' restroom was flooded as well. Any deeper and I could paddle a canoe through. I quickly dove into the water and turned off all the toilets in both restrooms. I prayed that I hadn't created this disaster. I wedged my head under the toilet I had worked on, and sure enough I spotted that the hairline crack I had originally detected was now the size of a crater. There was no escaping it. I was the culprit. Now there were no toilets available to any of the staff.

The boss very reluctantly made an announcement to all personnel stating that he'd be pleased to share his private, executive one stall upstairs bathroom with the entire staff until the others were repaired. He also stated that he'd found a competent plumber to come out shortly.

I sheepishly met with the boss in his office and confessed to what had happened. I said it could have happened to anyone. It was just bad luck. He stated that there was no need

The Cheap Handyman

to rush back to my department as I'd be spending the next couple of hours mopping up the mess I created. He also mentioned that there would be a serious shortage of hours for me in the coming months.

Estimated cost of job: $40

Actual cost of job: Huge loss of income

## Episode 19

**BUMPER TO BUMPER**

I love old cars, and when the opportunity arose to buy a 1948 MGA convertible, I jumped at the chance. It was a classic, and there weren't very many of them around anymore. A rare find indeed! I enjoyed working on cars, and with my self-proclaimed abundance of skills I was going to park this beauty in my garage and tinker with it until it was running like a well-oiled old watch. I could hardly wait! The only problem was that it needed some immediate attention, such as new brakes—there were no functioning brakes at all. Since it was a car I wasn't familiar with yet, I didn't want to experiment with something as important as brakes. I thought it best to have a professional mechanic do this repair. The last thing I'd need at this point was to mess with the brakes myself and have them fail on me. The problem was I'd have to somehow get the car from point A to point B without driving it.

It was only a short distance to travel, and I wasn't going to pay the exorbitant flat rate a towing company would charge. My mechanic buddy suggested that I grab a chain and have a friend use his car to tow the vehicle to the repair shop. Even though there were no brakes, as long as I had the car in

80

gear I could pump the clutch in and out as necessary and it would slow the car accordingly. In essence, it worked under the same principle as the brake. Of course, the trick was to carefully watch the car doing the towing, and when his brake lights came on I should immediately work the clutch. If I was too slow to respond, then metal might be meeting metal.

I was reluctant to ask any friend to help me out, but one did kindly volunteer. He was a longtime friend and we had helped each other out for years, so he didn't really have a problem coming to my rescue. He did want reassurance that this plan would work as he had a relatively new Dodge Charger. I said this idea came straight from the mechanic's mouth. He was fine with that. We both knew that this escapade would take precision and coordination, but we were up for it. I borrowed a hefty chain and we secured it to the frame under his back bumper. The other end was attached to the front frame of my car with about ten feet of slack in the middle. We were now good to go.

To avoid traffic and the police who would surely ticket us for this unorthodox mode of towing, we decided to take the back roads and cloak our move under the darkness of night. With both of us a bit nervous, he slowly moved forward until the slack was taken up and then sped up a bit. I felt a slight jolt, but we were on our way. As he sped up and slowed down, I adjusted my speed accordingly by pumping on the clutch. My car responded as needed. The mechanic was a smart guy! All was going well until we ran into one of those yellow light situations. Do you go or do you stop? I assumed as we were delicately towing a vehicle with a chain that he'd go through the light. Instead he slammed on his brakes. My eyes opened to the size of saucers and I hit the clutch as hard as I could. My car started to slow down, then the clutch went right to the floor, and I was no longer stopping.

The noise was deafening. I rammed into him so hard that both of his taillights exploded. I pushed him forward about four feet. The chain tightened and yanked me forward for a second time, knocking off his entire bumper and crumpling his trunk lid in the process. I was sick. I ricocheted back one last time and assaulted him again. On this impact, I dislodged his exhaust pipe, and it just hung there with no place to go. Sometime during the crashes, my front bumper and a few other unknown parts hit the ground. Remarkably neither of us had any blood pouring from our heads. We surveyed the damage. His car was substantially more banged up than mine. He was mighty red in the face.

It wasn't long before we heard the police siren, and our friends arrived within seconds. The officer listened to my pathetic analysis of this event and awarded me with two tickets. He then called for a tow truck and said I could pick my car up at the police pound, for a fee. He said the same to my friend.

We took a taxi home in silence.

**Estimated cost of repairs:  $250**

**Actual cost of repairs:  $2,900**

*Episode 20*

L ike any puppy, our beloved Patches had boundless energy and always wanted to play. The first few toys we bought him he ripped apart in seconds and had to be thrown out. Each toy was at least $15, and it would grind my gears that they only lasted a short period of time. Whether a brown squeaky weasel or his three-foot-long blue snake, we never got our money's worth out of any of them. Very early in this game, it became evident that I would be throwing a steady stream of money into toys that weren't worth it. I thought I'd just make some toys for him from things we had around the house. Wasn't like the little fella would know the difference.

I found a dilapidated mini football lying around in the garage. It was in a box with other sports stuff, which I kept as memories from when the kids were younger. The rubber on it had started to crack and break apart, but it would make an excellent toy. He was too young to be fetching the ball just yet, so I decided to poke two holes into it, thread a piece of rope through it, and use it for tug-of-wars and so on. I grabbed a metal coat hanger, cut the metal, and straightened it out so that I had a long metal wire. I taped one end of the string to the end of the wire, poked it through one hole, fished around, and poked it through the other hole. I then tied several knots in the end of the string so that it could not come back through the hole. I was ready to roll.

We had a blast with this homemade invention. I think I was having more fun than Patches. I had made the string about ten feet long so I could throw the ball quite a distance. He'd chase it, roll on it, grab the end of it with his little mouth, and start a tug-of-war. He was a happy little guy. As time went on, the games became a little more adventurous. I would then start throwing the ball a bit, have it land on the couch or chair, and he'd chase it, struggle to climb up, and then pounce on it. He always had both eyes glued to the ball, waiting for the next game to begin. To add a new dimension to our games, at one point I started swinging the string above my head. The football started circling, gaining more speed with each cycle. It reminded me of a cowboy with a swirling lasso, about ready to be hurled at a steer. The circling ball was moving at a good speed when suddenly it broke free of the string and flew across the room, smashed through the glass door of my wife's inherited antique china cabinet, and shattered numerous pieces of her Waterford crystal. This crystal was from Ireland, collector's items really, and outrageously expensive. Most of the pieces had been specially designed for us, one of a kind, and irreplaceable. I crapped myself twice, right on the spot.

Slouched over, I made my way to the cabinet. It, too, was very special, and old, having been given to us by my mother-in-law. The glass was broken, the fancy handle busted, and the decorative wooden framework broken in several places. The Waterford crystal, which even I had to admit was impressive, was lying in scattered bundles on the shelf. It was so smashed up that I couldn't be sure how many pieces had been totaled. Even one piece was one too many. My wife was so proud of this crystal. Sure as I had just shattered her collection, I was about to shatter her heart with this news.

My wife wasn't expected home for about an hour, so it gave me a little time to down as many drinks as possible. Nothing I had destroyed in the past came even close to this. The time I borrowed her car and smashed it up didn't hold a candle to this. I was in a store parking lot and didn't see the guy in front of me pull out of his parking spot. I broadsided him and caved in my wife's front bumper, among other things. It was the car she'd wanted her entire life and really didn't want me driving it. I knew that if a choice ever had to be made between her car and me, I would be long gone.

The fear I'd felt going home that day paled in comparison to the horror I felt waiting for my wife to come home now. When she arrived, I intercepted her on the porch. I wanted to talk with her before she could see anything. I asked her to sit down as I had something very important to say to her. She fell silent and had that worried look on her face I'd seen many times before: her jaw dropped and her eyebrows rose, her eyes locked open and stared into space. She thought someone had died or had been in a bad accident. When I confessed what had happened, I wished I *had* been in a bad accident and heavily drugged in a hospital somewhere. After a couple hours of grieving over the broken items and cabinet, and giving me the silent treatment, she started to calm down. She had calculated that about $6,000 worth of the exquisite glass had been destroyed. She had, however, figured out a solution to this crisis. Once a year, starting right now, we would be traveling overseas and purchasing, one by one, pieces of Waterford crystal of her choice, no matter the cost, until we had replenished what was lost.

I didn't want to sleep with my eyes open the rest of my life in fear of revenge if I said no, so I agreed. Patches, on the other hand, oblivious to the whole thing, was just tossing up and catching the football. He was dancing in the end zone.

**Estimated cost of toy:** $0

**Actual cost of toy:** $1,200 and counting; plus overseas flights (incalculable)

*Episode 21*

I was chugging along the road in a well-seasoned, rust-infested, rented stake truck. I would have preferred a much better one, of course, but this was the only one available and I couldn't wait another day for a replacement. It was an oldie with a twenty-five-foot box and it had great height. It guzzled so much gas that I became familiar with almost every gas station I passed. Like many rented trucks that have been overworked, it squeaked and rattled its way down the road. This particular one pulled constantly to the left and shook like crazy at more than thirty miles per hour. I was concerned that one of the wheels might just unbolt itself and roll off to the side at some point. It felt like I was riding in a covered wagon. Nonetheless, it would serve the purpose I needed it to. It would have been nice though if the radio had more than one functioning station as I had a fairly long trip ahead of me. I was on a furniture run.

See, we were having an issue with our bedroom set. Each piece was a relic and in constant need of repair. I thought I had performed the necessary repairs sufficiently, but my wife disagreed. Over the years, I had glued back on pieces of wood that had fallen off from too much slamming of the drawers. There was sanding done here and there where friction of moving parts had started to occur. These repairs of mine had been successful and kept the furniture in good working order for many years. Success stories didn't occur that often, which is why I felt quite hurt by my wife's harsh comments about my shoddy work. However, the wooden tracks for the drawers, which I had replaced numerous times, had put my wife over the top. They were now around twenty years old. I had replaced all of them for each dresser drawer. They were consistently sticking and jammed easily. The final straw was the cracked dresser leg: the cedar had split from dragging the dresser around the room instead of lifting it. The leg now angled out, which made the dresser lean to one side, and the leg was ready to give up the ghost at any time. My wife had had enough of my handiwork and wanted an entire new bedroom set, including two dressers, a mirror, two end tables, lamps, a bed frame, headboard, and a few other things I'd never even heard of. She'd found exactly what she wanted in a store about a hundred miles away. This store didn't deliver, but it did contract with an outside trucking company to do their deliveries. When I called to get a quote, his price was so high that I'd be better off renting a truck and picking up the new stuff myself. In the end, I arranged it with the store that I would use my own truck, they would load the furniture at their end, and I'd unload it at my end.

The next day I jumped into the very large stake truck, hit the highway, and arrived at my destination about an hour and a half later. Thirty minutes passed, the new items were padded, loaded, and tightly secured, and I was heading home. It was actually a pleasant drive aside from the nonstop rattling and bouncing of the truck, which was so violent it shifted my kidneys. It was far from driving my own pickup, which ran so smoothly on the highway it reminded me of a canoe gliding effortlessly through calm water. I arrived at my doorstep in good time and had my neighbor help me unload the truck. It was uneventful. Surprising since, knowing me, something usually went wrong. But somehow, we hadn't dropped or busted a single thing. My wife was delighted, everything fit in the bedroom, and I reassured myself that I had done the right thing.

Feeling damn good about myself I grabbed a bite to eat and then headed to a gas station to fill up before returning the truck. As I pulled into the lot and drove slowly toward the pumps, I noticed the gas attendant and other customers staring at me. *Strange.* When I was just a few feet away from the pumps, the six or so people standing around pumping gas bolted, scattering in all directions like rats fleeing from a sinking ship. *Did a bomb go off or something?* I was bewildered by their behavior until *BANG!* The intensity of the impact made me jam on the brakes. I could hear something grinding above me and shortly afterward saw chunks of cement bouncing off the hood of the truck. I rammed the truck into park and jumped out without even turning off the engine just in time to see that the top three feet of the truck box was crumpled and securely wedged under the overhang of the gas station.

Clearly it had never crossed my mind that the truck was too tall for the overhang. I could see stress cracks forming throughout all the cement. I immediately broke into a sweat. The lump in my throat had risen about three inches, and the sudden scare just about made me have a bladder malfunction.

Ashamed and embarrassed, I watched in horror as the stress cracks fissured through the cement. A crowd was forming and pointing, which made things even worse. The police raced into the station with sirens and lights blazing, followed quickly by the fire trucks and ambulance. The police cordoned off the station with yellow caution tape as if it were a crime scene. Over in the corner the ambulance was setting up to treat people who showed signs of heart palpitations. I was mortified.

The police had zoomed in on me from the first second they arrived. I guess it was my red, guilty face that gave me away. I was immediately put in the back of the police car and told not to leave the vehicle. As if I could leave—the doors automatically locked. I looked through the wire fencing separating the front and back seats as the officers started interviewing people who had witnessed this debacle. I felt like I had been put into an isolation cell in a maximum-security prison. It seemed like several hours before they returned. I thought they had forgotten about me. I was exhausted by the time I answered all their questions. I admitted that it was all my fault and was charged with careless driving and a few lesser offences.

Eventually, they let me go, and left. Looking at the truck

bonded to the overhang I realized that I had to get it out and back to the rental company. I tried to back it out, but in doing so a ten-foot stretch of the overhang in front of me broke apart and plummeted to the ground. Still, the truck didn't move.

A few spectators who felt sorry for me came over, stood beside me, and offered their ideas on how to resolve this most difficult problem. From calling a tow truck and yanking the sad old junker out to just gunning the thing out in reverse, I felt the best solution was to let most of the air out of the tires and have a load-full of people stand in the back of the truck, weigh it down, and hopefully reverse it out. That worked, but what a disaster!

Finally, after being disgraced in front of the entire station, I was allowed to head out. I hardly relished the thought of showing the truck to the rental company and telling them what had happened. I'd immediately slap down the $1,000 collision deductible if it meant I could slip away quickly and quietly into the darkness.

**Estimated cost of trip:** $250

**Actual cost of trip:** $1,550; numerous humongous tickets; plus disgrace and a lifetime of shame

*Episode 22*

## THE CRAWL SPACE

### CAT-ASTROPHE

The beginning of November always marked the start of winterizing for me. It was time to put lawn furniture away and make sure that I had put gas stabilizer in the lawn mower and pressure washer. If I didn't, the gas would become stale over the winter and need to be drained and replaced with fresh gas next spring—an absolute pain in the butt. These machines would never start up with old gas. Of course, it took me years to figure this out. I'd yank the cord on these damn machines until I just about dislocated my shoulder, and still they wouldn't start. By the time I was finished my knuckles were dragging on the ground. It wasn't until I paid $100 to a wise old guy at a repair shop that I learned all I had to do was get rid of the old gas. He said that was all he did.

Winterizing also meant it was time to make my twice-yearly foray into the crawl space to shut off the water for the outside hose. This time of year, the weather started to turn ugly and cold. If the temperature dropped too much there was always the risk of pipes freezing. Cracked pipes were costly to replace. As our house had a crawl space, the pipes were much more exposed to the weather conditions than homes with a

92

proper basement. When we bought the house about twenty years ago, I had been too cheap to have an outside shut-off valve installed, so I'd have to manually do this job, which I absolutely hated. Bugs and spiders crawled over me every step of the way, with the odd mouse coming almost nose to nose with me out of curiosity. No point complaining, just get going.

I would always have to fall into the dark pit of the crawl space. It was so dark that I had to use a flashlight to find my way. I felt there were a hundred eyes on me. There was so little room to move that I had to suck in my gut so as not to get it stuck on one of the support beams. It was thirty feet of agony dragging myself to reach the shut-off valve. And the whole time all I could think of was getting stuck there and being left for dead. I did, however, get the job done. I was covered in filth from head to toe and had sweated off about five pounds, but at least I wouldn't have to do this again until the spring. I secured the piece of plywood that covered the opening to the crawl space with six screws—one in each corner and two in the middle of the wooden framework surrounding the plywood. It didn't look pretty, but it did the job. The opening was tightly sealed. Life was good!

The next day I was watching TV when I heard a noise coming from under the house. It sounded like some kind of animal moving around. Going back into that damn crawl space reminded me of the last root canal I had, but I had to investigate that strange sound. I manned up, grabbed my flashlight, and headed down under. There in the far back I spotted her: a huge, black and white, and very pregnant cat hiding in the corner. She must have snuck into the crawl space while I was turning off the water and I had accidentally locked her in. I approached her slowly, but with a few quick near misses of her claws I could see she wasn't going to come quietly. Fair enough, she was frightened. I made a few calls to the animal rescue people for assistance, thinking they would have all kinds of good ideas for me, but unfortunately they basically said that I was on my own and good luck! They were sympathetic to my cause, but none could come out for at least a week. I couldn't leave the poor cat in peril for that long, so I'd perform the rescue myself. I went and bought cat treats and toys, and I even tried coaxing her out with a song or two, but nothing would entice her to come out. I set out bowls with food and water near the exit, hoping she'd come close enough that I could grab her, but two days later we were still at a standoff.

On the third morning my wife and I were having coffee in the kitchen, when we heard a faint scraping noise coming from the floor, followed by what sounded like a soft meowing. All of a sudden, the floor vent started to rise up, and out popped the head of a tiny kitten, black and white with a touch of orange. I just about needed a change of underwear. Mother had obviously delivered her babies, but how the hell did they get in the duct work? And what do I do now? Flashlight in hand, back to the dark pit I went.

I scanned the crawl space with my light looking for the family. Most of the duct work was metal but some was made out of fabric. It was a pliable material that could be used for very sharp corners and tight spaces where metal would be difficult to install. I could see that Mother, in an act of desperation, had ripped a large hole in it, looking for an escape route. What a catastrophe! Cats running everywhere! It looked to me like there were seven in total. All we could think to do was entice the little critters with food at the entrance of the crawl space and hope the entire troop would leave the premises. Not one reared a head. We then removed each of the nine floor vents in the house and placed food there. Again, no takers. All we could do was try to wait them out.

I reflected that for a very small amount of money, I could have had a shut-off water valve installed outside the house and avoided all this drama. Now I had to pay the rescuers, pay for someone to repair the duct work, and pay for someone to fumigate all the duct work in the house. Our series of metal tunnels was like a massive playground for the young bucks. They could play all day long and pee and drop loads whenever they wanted. They would have a blast in there! Unfortunately, it would just be a matter of time before unfavorable smells would start to drift up the vents, especially in the winter when we turned the heat on. The ripped fabric material would certainly have to be repaired as the holes there would let heat and cold air escape, which would inevitably result in higher bills.

I was back on the phone with animal control. My attempts to rescue the cats had failed and if I didn't prod these people a bit, it may take them weeks to show up. The longer the delay, the more damage that could be done. More important, I was an animal lover and very concerned about the cats being stuck in a cold crawl space for too long. The guys must have heard the desperation in my begging, as I was able to talk them into coming out the next day.

I must say I was impressed with how quickly and professionally they got all the cats out. Expecting it would take a while and not wanting to get caught up in all the action, I disappeared and had a nap. But not two hours later they knocked at the door and said they were leaving. Mother and all kittens accounted for with no casualties. They must have used some magical spell or something to complete that task so quickly. They were, of course, the experts!

**Estimated cost of job: $75**

**Actual cost of job: $650**

*Episode 23*

## THE COVER UP

The upside of having a pool was taking off the cover as summer loomed just around the corner. It meant that good times were not far away. The downside of having a pool was closing it up in the fall. Winter would be knocking on the door before too long, and it seemed like we'd have to wait forever to enjoy the pool again.

The pool had one of those thick, heavy plastic covers that dips in about four feet and snaps into a track that surrounds the perimeter of the pool. As the pool people charged so much to winterize it and put on the cover, I did the winterizing myself, and my wife and I put on the cover. I was quite used to lowering the water level to below the jets, blowing out the lines and winterizing them. Still, it was never a pleasant job putting on that cover, but we did get it done. Or, at least, we did until this year. After struggling for hours with that monster, my wife begged me to call the experts. Naturally, I refused. We just needed a little more man power, that's all. The cover was now close to a decade old and not as flexible as before, but it was still perfectly doable. As in many past instances, I called over my loyal friends to assist us.

There were now five of us in total. It was always the same with my buddies. Two of them would arrive dressed as if they had just stepped out of a storm sewer, while the other guy would show up dressed quite immaculately. He always wore expensive clothes, shoes, and accessories. I called him out on that once, and he replied that he "didn't really want to dress way down" to my level. I left it at that.

We spaced ourselves around the pool, an equal distance from one another, and grabbed on to the liner. We then lifted it up and walked around the pool until the cover was aligned with the kidney shape of the pool. The plan was for all of us to pull on the cover simultaneously and hook the cover in the track in a few key spots and then do the rest of it. That plan didn't work, and we ended up all yanking at the same time with no results. It quickly became apparent that the cover had shrunk substantially since last year. It became a tug-of-war contest, with each side trying to be the victor, until the guy beside me and I pulled so hard that my well-dressed friend was violently catapulted forward and twisted in the air. He did a backward swan dive into the deep end of the pool and slid on his back down the liner and into the freezing water, oxfords and all. We could hear the splash and scream as the water broke his fall. We all rushed over, and once we saw he was fine we broke into laughter. There were no ladders on the pool at this point, so we had to pull him out like a stranded walrus. Sopping wet, he kicked off his expensive dress shoes and took off his Rolex watch, which he informed me was no longer ticking. He had lost his designer sunglasses somewhere in the pool. We scooped them out with the pool net and then scooped around again until we found the one arm of his glasses that had broken off during his nosedive. The glasses were bent with one lens gone. He was not impressed. My other buddies and wife, who had been an unwilling participant in this venture, read the signs quickly and made a beeline for the house.

I had faced the music many times in the past. Like the time I borrowed my buddy's MasterCraft boat. I miscalculated my speed as I approached the dock and slammed into it, cracking the fiberglass hull. I thought he was going to have a stroke when I told him, but by the next summer he was talking to me again. And I'll never forget when a close friend loaned me his newly bought, right out of the box, compressor. I was impressed that he thought enough of me to trust me with his new toy. I gassed it up and yanked the cord. It purred. After about five minutes, though, it started coughing and gagging and just stopped. I couldn't get it going again. I then thought it might be a good time to read the instructions. In bold print on the first page it stated, "DON'T FORGET TO PUT IN THE OIL." The compressor was now toast. Shamefully, I shared my sad story with my maybe-no-longer friend and pulled out a wad of cash for him to buy a new one. No warranty on earth would cover such low brain activity. I don't hear from him too much anymore!

But in this case, I really didn't know how to handle the situation. To be honest, I still found the whole thing very comical, but he wasn't laughing. If I had been in his place,

I would have said no big deal, as I only have a trash watch, cheap shoes, and even cheaper sunglasses. I waited for him to make the first move. After a moment of contemplation, he said best friends or not, I'd have to replace his stuff and it would be from stores that I had never even heard of. Not much I could do but agree. After all, the man had in good faith offered his services free, and I had cost him something in the process. I now had to wait in fear for the receipts. The following day I called the pool people and booked a pool closing appointment.

**Estimated cost of job: $0**

**Actual cost of job: $2,800**

## Episode 24

**BLADE RUNNER**

I love hockey. What can I say? I'm Canadian. I have played it all my life, from when I was a very young kid through my school years, and still going strong now. It means a great deal to me. I was past the days of thinking I was a star, but that didn't stop my buddies and me from playing twice a week. Not only was it some exercise, but the boys and I always went out for some beers afterward and told over and over again the stories we've heard a hundred times before. We still laughed just as hard as the first time we'd heard them. We had known one another for many years and had started up a tournament team long ago. We especially enjoyed playing in the organized tournaments.

The season had just begun, and our very first game was against a team that had beaten us every time in the past. We were hoping to change that this time around. I pulled my equipment out of its summer storage place in the garage and opened it up. The months of heat had only enhanced its mellow fragrance. The fumes just about knocked me off my feet. I had never been one to take good care of my equipment.

Unlike my tools, which I kept in mint condition and meticulously free of rust, washing my gear perhaps once every year or two was more than sufficient for me. Most of these guys tossed any equipment that could be washed into the washer at least once a month, but I didn't think that was necessary. My buddies used to sit on the other side of the dressing room and had constantly pleaded with me to toss out that load of stench and buy some new stuff. Hockey equipment was outrageously expensive, and I wasn't going to lay out that kind of dough. I'd just have to milk it. Besides, this equipment and I had history.

It was game time, and we fought like dogs to get a one-goal lead by the end of the first period. The second period was relatively uneventful, until I made a sharp circle in our end and the entire blade holder on my left skate fell off. The blade was still intact. I went down and slid as if I were gunning for home plate in the World Series. Thankfully I wasn't hurt. Inspecting the sole of my skate boot, I could see that it was so rotten and mold infested there was nothing left to hold the blade holder onto the sole. I had an anxiety attack on the spot, as I feared that was it for me. I wouldn't be able to finish the game. I was pissed until I saw someone running up with a roll of duct tape. I held the skate boot while another guy began wrapping the tape through the blade holder and then around the boot. He was able to do it in three different spots. He wrapped it as tightly as possible, leaving only enough room for my foot to fit inside. I put my skate back on and walked around a bit. I was a bit nervous as there was definitely a wobble present, but if I didn't push too hard off my left foot, all should be fine. I was now back in the lineup.

The third period started with the other team scoring a few seconds into it. We were now tied. On the ice I cruised around, not really applying myself unless absolutely necessary. Unexpectedly, one of their defensemen fell and I was passed the puck. I now had a breakaway. I turned on the jets, and twenty feet from the goalie I gave one last push off with my left foot. The blade holder bent totally sideways and dragged along the ice. I swerved erratically across the rink like a car that had just blown a tire. Lifting my head and trying desperately to regain control, I saw the referee right in front of me, leaning against the boards. I raised my stick instinctively and unintentionally cross-checked him in the chest. He went to the ice like a rock. Within seconds the paramedic on duty was looking down at him and calling for an ambulance. I watched them carry him off on a stretcher.

The next day I went to the hospital to visit the poor guy. I even thought of bringing flowers, but quickly realized that it wasn't something a macho hockey player like me would do. His family members were talking outside of his room. When they saw me, they immediately stood in front of the doorway. I tried to explain what had happened and that it was just an accident, but they weren't interested in listening. I did find out from the nurse that he was actually all right but being kept in overnight for observation. I still felt terrible.

The next day I was called in by the hockey league review

board. It didn't take long for the tribunal to suspend me for the remainder of the season and tack on a fine. I pleaded with them not to suspend me as the season had just begun and to double or triple the fine, I didn't care. They listened and then suggested that I carry my hockey bag back to the garage and hang it up.

**Estimated cost of hockey:** $0

**Actual cost of hockey:** $400 and a very long, boring winter

## Episode 25

## RAMP IT UP

**S**now on the ground meant it was time to store my motorcycle for the winter. I had an older 110cc Yamaha in those days, which I really enjoyed riding. It was quick, and I loved cruising through the country roads. The only drawback was that it was heavy and a bit difficult to ride. Most bikes had a seat that was lower to the ground than mine was. A lower seat meant a lower center of gravity, which made it easier to control the machine. My seat sat right on the top of the bike. It was like sitting on a piece of plywood. On long rides I'd have to get off the bike frequently and rearrange my bone structure before I could get back on it. I often had to fight with the bike to get it to do what I wanted, but nonetheless, my Yamaha and I had a solid relationship. I always found it too expensive to pay for storage, so I thought I'd simply store it in my large shed at the back of the yard. There was a one-foot step up into the shed, so I'd have to make a ramp to drive it up—no problem.

I carefully drove my bike up to the entrance of the shed to suss things out. Eyeballing the situation, I noticed that the width of the door and the width of the bike handlebars were not that different. I got out my tape measure and concluded that the handlebars were about two inches narrower than the opening. It would be tight, but with steady hands and lined up perfectly I could guide this baby into its winter home.

Making a suitable ramp to drive the bike up didn't seem that difficult. Once again, I viewed a few tell-all videos and felt confident. They basically showed a slightly sloped ramp made of plywood the width of the door opening that was attached to the bottom of that opening with the other end lying on the grass. It looked relatively easy to build. Looked like all I needed to buy was a 5/8-inch-thick, four-by-eight piece of plywood, some black nonslip tape, and a couple of two-by-fours. All excited, I drove to the neighborhood hardware store, purchased the plywood, and had them cut it to the specs of the door opening. I also bought the nonslip tape, brought it home, and applied it to the wood. I secured one end of the plywood to the base of the door opening and allowed the other end to fall freely onto the grass. It looked like a million bucks! The only thing I hadn't done was put the two-by-fours under the ramp for added support. It had been strongly recommended, but since I'd forgotten to buy it, I'd go without it.

I pulled my bike up to the shed, revved it up like a kid with a new toy, and deliberated on things one more time before starting. I lined the bike up as best I could with the center of the door opening, about five feet behind the ramp. Like the pros, I dropped my head for a moment, concentrated on what I was going to do, as I was a bit nervous, and then raised my head with full confidence. I hit the gas and sprinted up the ramp. To my surprise the middle of the ramp dipped like a bow flexing, and before I knew it, I bounced up like a crazy man on a trampoline and became slightly airborne. That unexpected lift changed my trajectory, causing the bike to veer right. The one handlebar smacked directly into the right side of the door jam and brought the bike to a dead halt. It sent me over the handlebars and landed me flat on my back in the middle of the shed floor. I lay there stunned for a few moments, looking up at the insulation on the ceiling. I wasn't really sure if I'd just had a bad dream or if this had really happened. Apparently, those extra two-by-fours were more important than I had thought. I should have gone back and picked some up and placed them under the center of the ramp for further support, as I was instructed to do. With that added support I would have smoothly sailed directly into the shed. I eventually got myself right side up and ventured to the door.

The bike was half lying on its side with the handlebars turned sideways, and the front of the bike was securely wedged in the door opening. The front bumper was mangled and sticking straight up. Somehow the seat had dislodged itself and was lying on the ground a few feet away. There were pieces of fallen bike parts scattered around the door opening. This bike needed to be put out of its misery. I felt like I was going to toss my cookies!

It took four big guys about half an hour to dislodge the bike from the shed and cart it off to the dealership. It was gut-wrenching to hear the metal being twisted and turned. The $100 per month storage charge didn't seem that bad right now.

**Estimated cost of job: $75**

**Actual cost of job: $1,800**

*Episode 26*

Part of our house had a second story with a small overhang outside the patio door. It must have been an afterthought by the builder because it was as utterly useless as it was dangerous. In the first place, the overhang was only about three feet by three feet and not that sturdy. I had nightmares about stepping out onto it, dropping straight through like a rock, and snapping both ankles on the cement deck below. And now, it leaked. Of course, thanks to my vivid imagination, I was hesitant to go out on a limb to fix a leak. We had another patio door directly below the one on the second floor. When it rained, water would just pool on that overhang, and over time it had found a path down to the ceiling of the main floor. It would run along the top of the patio door and just drip incessantly onto the floor. If you sat there long enough your foot would start tapping to the beat of the drops. I had no doubt that the caulking at the base of the second story door had dried out and cracked and needed replacing. I didn't even bother getting quotes this time. This handyman would have the repair work done in no time.

Before I stepped one toe onto that death trap of a ledge,

109

I made sure I had my toolbox with me, along with a new tube of silicone caulking and a caulking gun. I glanced at my hammer, The Beast, and nodded—you never knew when it would be called into action. It was such a small area to work on that once I plunked my butt on the ledge, there was hardly any room to move around, so I'd have to be extremely careful. I remember when I had to put a new protective surface on that ledge ten years before. I went all out and put down an EPDM (ethylene polypropylene diene monomer) membrane. It was rubberized and one inch thick and guaranteed to outlive me. Once cut to size, it was secured to the ledge with nails. Silicone was then put over the nail heads to keep water out. The same silicone was used to seal up the joint between where the membrane and the bottom of the patio door met. My chore today was to replace the silicone and hopefully stop the leak. I could see where that bead of silicone had been beaten up by the weather. Most of it had dried right out and cracked and some sections had just blown away. I assembled around me what I'd need for this task: utility knife, screwdriver, caulk, caulking gun, and several rags. It really wasn't that big a job. I used my screwdriver to pick out the remaining parts of the old bead of caulk and laid down a new similar bead. I double checked to make sure I hadn't missed any spots, and I was done. This particular type of silicone offered instant protection even if it started raining immediately, so there was none of this praying it didn't rain until the silicone dried.

By now my body had stiffened up. I had to pull my legs straight out from under me, crack my knees a few times to get them moving, and massage my ankles to get some blood flowing down there. In the process of bringing my body back to life, I stretched out my one leg and watched as it caught The Beast, pushing it off the side of the ledge. It was a heavy hammer and it disappeared from sight in an instant. I knew it had come to a stop when I heard the sound of glass breaking. I peered over the side of the ledge to see that The Beast had landed solidly on the corner of the glass top of the patio table. I froze for a second and then hoofed it down to the poolside. The hammer had only put a fairly large hairline crack in the very corner of the top, but it was nothing that some duct tape couldn't fix. My wife wasn't home at the time, so I made haste and grabbed the magical tape, cut it just slightly wider than the splinter, and surgically covered it up. From time to time my wife had the ability of not noticing the obvious, and I was counting on it this time around. It would take a very keen eye to spot the blemish.

It was only seconds after my wife arrived home that I was interrogated about the damage to the table. I don't know how she zoomed in on the mishap so quickly. At first I said this was news to me, but I retracted my statement just as quickly. She could always tell when I was hiding something from her—I'd start to sweat and become silent. I confessed and said that the repair job was more than sufficient. She disagreed!

We had spared nothing in purchasing a top-quality patio set to add additional ambience to the pool scene. This particular tabletop was solid glass and one-half inch thick. I knew it was expensive as it took two people to lift it. The table and chairs had that rich look about them. The paint on the table was a dark gray with speckles of dark yellow mixed in. It reminded me of the paint you'd see on a high-end car. There were six chairs, and they were the most comfortable I'd ever sat in. The back and seat were covered with soft mesh and could rock you to sleep if you so desired. It was a sharp-looking patio set. I knew there would probably be a sharper-looking price attached to the glass replacement the second time around.

**Estimated cost of the job: $6.95**

**Actual cost of the job: $275**

*Episode 27*

We were young, not married for very long, and free of owning a home or having kids, as of yet. It was a perfect time in our lives to take some chances. We decided to move from one end of the country to the other, find new jobs, and enjoy life while we could. It would be a four-day road trip. We didn't really have a lot of furniture of our own, but the cost to have professional movers transport it to our new home was way more than I wanted to pay. We decided to trade in our old vehicle on a used cargo van.

The van seemed large enough when we first purchased it, but as we started packing our things in, it felt like it was getting smaller all the time. I could have used an engineering degree as I had to pack, unload, pack, and unpack again, again and again until we were able to get everything in. There was hardly enough room for our old companion, Sylvester the cat. We had never gone anywhere without him. He was family! Finally, I slammed the back doors shut, and to be sure they stayed closed I tied the two door handles together with rope. We were ready to hit the road and seek out new adventures!

The only negative thing about this trip was the timing of

113

our departure. We were spontaneous and had decided at the last second to make this move, not thinking about the fact that it was winter. It was a long trip, so we took turns driving. We would plunk ourselves in a hotel each night after a full day of traveling. We hardly ever saw Sylvester during the day. He had a hideout somewhere in the back with all the stuff and only surfaced when it was time to take him into the hotel. The weather was frigid from the moment we left, but it had never snowed.

We were now on our fourth day and about eight hours from our destination. The first three days just flew by. We talked about where we hoped to find an apartment, what jobs we would look for, and what kind of a new life we wanted to build for ourselves. It was all very exciting. My wife was always up for new challenges. This was the most difficult day as we were now driving through beautiful but dangerous mountainous terrain, and it was really snowing. It was so cold that the water in the cat's bowl had frozen. We couldn't see him and could only hope that he wasn't a frozen slab somewhere in the back of the van.

We made considerably slower time than expected and found ourselves at the top of a winding mountain road, in the dark, when we got a flat tire. It was panic time. There was absolutely no traffic on this road, so the chance of a rescue was slim, and the snow was blowing so fiercely that it was unlikely anyone would even see us. I had no choice but to grab the jack, change the tire, and pray that I didn't freeze to death in the process. It was the back tire on the passenger side and very tricky to work on as it was very close to where the shoulder ended and a huge drop began. One too many steps backward and I'd never be seen again.

As I started to jack up the van, I noticed that the jack had a serious curve in it. As I jacked it up more, the bend became larger. The jack was made to handle the weight of the van, but not a van filled to the gills with heavy furniture. I lowered the jack and then started throwing stuff out of the back and into the snow bank. I first made sure that Sylvester was safe and secure in my wife's arms or he may have been chucked out as well. I ended up dumping our complete furniture set on the side of the road, including the dressers, bed, bed frame, etc., along with our TV and stand. I then tried to change the tire again and was successful this time. I started loading the items back into the van I was rushing as it was so cold. I couldn't take the time to place the items back into their designated spots. I just started tossing things in. Before long the van looked full except for the fact that some of the bedroom set and a few other items were still on the road. It was too cold and dangerous to try to repack the vehicle again, so we decided to leave our possessions there and come back in the morning. Most likely no one would even be on this road.

We were up before the roosters the next day. We just left our stuff in our van and rented another. We wanted to make haste in retrieving our abandoned furniture. The storm had passed, so we made good time. We knew it wouldn't be hard to spot our things as they were in a big pile on the side of the road. We drove up and down where we thought we had dumped our cargo and didn't see anything. We expanded the search and still saw nothing. I knew we were in the right area. Looking to the shoulder as we cruised along, I saw something familiar. It was our TV stand. I jumped out and saw a note attached to it that said, "Thank you for the furniture, but we already have a TV stand." I was livid. The gall of someone to steal a poor man's belongings!

We got all set up in our new apartment. It looked incomplete in that we had a large dresser without the two smaller matching tables, no mirror for the top of the dresser, and a TV stand leaning against the wall, crying out for its TV. It was depressing. Thinking back, I probably could have squeezed my wallet a little more, paid for a moving company, and flown down in comfort. Painfully, now we would have to dig deep as we went furniture shopping.

And to add insult to injury, after all the drama we experienced and all the expenses incurred, a few months later we had decided this wasn't the place for us. We were going home. That first call we made was to a moving company.

**Estimated cost of trip: $600**

**Actual cost of trip: $3,300**

*Episode 28*

## BIKE RACK

## TRAIN WRECK

The summer had rolled around again at last, and we were about to take off on my favorite family vacation: camping. The kids and I particularly liked it. We loved getting away from the crazy city life for a bit and just enjoying nature at its best. They always enjoyed setting up and sleeping in the camper. They found that really cool. They could go to bed when they wanted and get up whenever they chose. We'd sit around the campfire at night, tell stories, and just laugh until our stomachs ached. We were not on any time schedule, which was such a pleasant change. For me, I just liked to plunk my butt in a chair at the edge of the lake. I'd listen to the birds or fall asleep or just stare into space. Sometimes late at night I'd just sit there and enjoy the silence. Not having to drive anywhere or be accountable for anything was more than I could ask for. My wife was from Ireland and had never experienced it growing up, but she was a good sport and always made the sacrifice to come with us. As was the case in past years, we had our fold-down camper trailer, which we towed behind the car. This year we were going to add a new dimension to our travels and bring our bicycles along. We were camping at a larger national park this year. It was a longer hike to get to than in past years, but we were told it had awesome bike trails.

We had never had any kind of bike racks in the past. At one time I had considered getting a bike rack that hooked into the trailer harness of the car, but since it could never be used if we were towing the camper, I passed on that idea. I had seen many people with the cool racks that were attached to the top of the camper unit. These racks would hold up to four bicycles; each bike had its own sleeve, which held it in an upright position. This was exactly what we needed, but I wasn't too keen on spending the money to get one. This was an experiment for us, after all, and if this trip ended up being anything but great, we might never use the rack again. Why waste money? My only solution was to call around and see if any of my buddies had such a rack that I could borrow.

I lucked out: my friend Ron, who used to be an avid cyclist, had an old one I could borrow. He was older than I was, and the nicest guy in the world. He had to stop riding due to arthritis in his shoulders, a knee replacement, back problems, a broken left wrist that never healed properly, and very poor eyesight. He was afraid that he might now self-destruct if he rode, so he hung up his bike for good—sad, really. I went over to his house to pick up the rack. He gave me fair warning that this was an older rack and hadn't, in all honesty, been used in years. We had to haul about thirty things out of his garage in order to reach the thing. We dragged it out and had a good look at it. It was 75 percent metal and 25 percent rust. I took particular notice of the welds where the vertical poles attached to the base of the rack and how much rust had accumulated there. The sleeves themselves were welded to the vertical poles and also looked like they were on their last legs. It had undoubtedly affected the integrity of the metal but was still salvageable in my opinion. I could spray on a ton of lubricant and scrub off a great deal of the rust. Then I would turn where every handyman turns in a pinch: duct tape. Duct tape was a marvelous invention! I had used it to hold together pipes, hold together my cars, and so many other things that would take me a day to list. It was a must for every toolbox!

At home, I got to work scouring off the rust, then started wrapping duct tape around just about every joint and weld. I think I used an entire roll of the stuff in the process and the rack looked hideous. Originally a black rack, it now looked like it had been in a serious accident and was about 50 percent bandaged together with gray duct tape. Still, it was as secure as it would ever be and, besides, it would be mounted on top of the trailer. Hardly anyone would see it. With the rack still on the garage floor, I loaded the three bikes into their allocated sleeves. Two of the bicycles were brand-new as our kids (now ten and twelve years old) had grown out of their old ones—and what better time to get them new bikes than on an exciting, new camping road trip! With all the bikes in place, I gave the rack a shake or two to assess its stability. The rack swayed side to side, but short of hurricane winds I felt that it would hold up. Operation Bike Rack was good to go.

The day we left was, as always, full of excitement. The kids packed their own stuff while I mounted the rack on the camper unit. It lay on top of the roof and was secured to the trailer by four tie-down ratchet straps, one in each corner. I tightened each strap to its limit and felt it was solid. It was a bit of a gut buster lifting the bikes up and into position, but in short order it was done, and we were on the road. Part of the trip was the journey to get there. We always sang, played games, and just gabbed about anything and everything. It was great. It seemed that in our everyday lives we were all so busy that we hardly had time to even talk with one another. On a trip like this we could let our hair down and catch up on what everyone was doing. It was an excellent time for some bonding.

Not too far from the park I pointed out the beautiful terrain to the family. We were now going through a very hilly area with steep ups and downs and winding roads. Some of the drops were so steep that there were guardrails on the shoulders. A great place to get rid of a body if necessary. Just drop it over the side and it would never be seen again. All was going well until I took one of the corners far too fast. I slammed on the brakes to regain control of the situation. As I was doing this, I heard a scraping noise from the camper behind me and noticed that the bikes were no longer on top of the trailer. I abruptly stopped and we ran back down the road. There was no sign of them. We looked over the guardrail and could not even see the bottom. Their brand-new, hardly ridden, shiny bikes and my old, dilapidated, beaten-up crap bike were long gone, never to be found. I was sick. I had no choice but to reassure the children that we'd buy them new bikes upon our arrival at the park.

I walked back to the car, tail between my legs. I looked up at the rack on the trailer. The base of it hadn't moved an inch but the entire vertical framework was gone. It must have bent all the way to one side when I took the corner too quickly. The stress from all that weight on one side had snapped the four main welds allowing the top part of the rack to fly off into the abyss. The bikes were just collateral damage. The duct tape had not done its job, and I was seriously considering removing it from my toolbox as I was no longer sure it could be considered one of my most reliable tools. I felt as if a longtime friend had just betrayed me, and it was going to take me some time to get over this. In reality, I should not have used that broken-down, ready-for-the-grave bike rack.

**Estimated cost of trip:** $25 0

**Actual cost of trip:** $780

*Episode 29*

## LIGHTS OUT

We had a good-sized backyard and decided to put in a beautiful in-ground pool. We had long dreamed of having one, and now that the dream was becoming reality we didn't spare a dime. It had extra cement around the perimeter, an attractive board-on-board wooden fence for privacy, and an aluminum no-maintenance-ever fence surrounding the rest of the pool. We had put in fancy walk-in steps, a diving board, a slide, a ladder in the deep end, and two spotlights of which I was particularly proud. At night these lights spread their glory across the entire pool and a blue glow could be seen from all angles. It was absolutely to die for. These gems were the highlight of the entire pool. My wife, kids, and I sat out there long into the summer nights, just taking in all the ambience. The pool was heated, which allowed us to just jump in whenever we felt the urge. We'd swim for hours and often never headed indoors until well after midnight. We were still enjoying this piece of heaven into our third year.

One night we were lounging around the pool and I noticed that one of the lights was not working. I was immediately in distress. I couldn't even sit still until I sorted this out.

I reached into the pool, untwisted the light, and pulled it out. The bulb must have been loose or there was a loose connection. I fiddled around with it for a few minutes, making sure there wasn't any rust on the bottom of it which could impede the connection to the socket, and shook it to make sure the filament inside the bulb wasn't broken. I didn't really find anything wrong, so I screwed it back into its socket. The light still didn't work. Then I went over to the fuse box, pulled out the tiny fuse, and examined it carefully. I didn't find a broken filament—which I had hoped was the case—and then replaced the fuse. Everything seemed in order. I turned it on again . . . still no change. I was really upset now. This light was ruining my whole evening. I had no choice but to call the pool company in the morning.

One of the pool installers came out the next day and repeated what I had done, with the same results. He said there must be a loose wire or a short somewhere in the electrical box. There must have been hundreds of wires in there, all crisscrossing and mashed together and connected to dozens of screws and clamps. It was mind-boggling. He got out his tester and started checking every wire he could find. After about an hour he scratched his head and said he couldn't find anything wrong. He said he was afraid it's just one of those crazy intermittent electrical problems and the source of it will probably never be found. I was just going to have live with it. And with that he packed up his stuff and left. I couldn't live with that answer. I called the company and they reiterated what their man had said. The pool was long out of its one-year warranty, our man did the best he could, and there was nothing else we could do for you. I was now on my own.

I kind of flew off the handle at this point. I did agree with the repairman that the problem was somewhere in the electrical box. But to leave this problem unresolved was like leaving half a steak dinner still on the plate. You just didn't do that! This was the pool of my dreams, and I wasn't going to just roll over and die. I'd investigate the problem myself. There had to be some small loose wire that was causing the problem, and I was going to find it.

I made a beeline back to the electrical box, opened the door, and stared at the mass of ganglia staring back at me. Where did I even start? I systematically undid each connection, one at a time, checked the end of the wire and screw for rust, and then securely tightened it back up. After about two hours, I determined that it would take approximately forever to get through all of them, so I decided to detached clusters of wires close to each other, being ever diligent in remembering what wire went where. I was able to cut my labor time in half, and after all was said and done I felt no wire or connection had been left untouched.

It was the moment of truth. I stood back and turned the power back on. Immediately sparks started to fly, and a small fire ensued. I stepped back instinctively, and not a moment too soon: not three inches in front of me a two-foot flame shot out of the top of the motor. It reminded me of a flame thrower. Had I been even one inch closer it would have singed my privates. A few seconds later the electrical box and motor were puffing out black smoke and then all was silent. So was I.

A few days later the same repairman, this time accompanied by two others, was back to begin the rebuilding process. The motor and electrical box were toast and just tossed to the side. All the wiring had to be replaced, and a new electrical box had to be installed along with a new motor. About three hours later they were done. He turned on the power and once again I could hear the purring of the motor and filter system. I wouldn't be purring much when the bill arrived. . . .

That night, to stem my curiosity, I strolled over to the pool light switch and snapped it on. I looked into the pool. The light still didn't work.

**Estimated cost of repairs:** $0

**Actual cost of repairs:** $800

## Episode 30

## TRAILER TRAGEDY

Our fridge was on the fritz and we needed to replace it. The ice cube maker had stopped working and the light in the main part of the fridge kept flashing on and off as if it were trying to send someone an SOS. Additionally, the motor now had quite a roar to it. It was not worth fixing. I saw an ad for a used one, checked it out, and purchased it on the spot. I now had to get it from there to my place, which was about a mile or so. I was not going to lay out dough on a rented van for such a short distance. I did own an old, weathered, beat-up trailer that I could put into action. In the past I had used it quite often to run things to the dump, but for the last few years it just sat there, dormant.

I pulled the trailer out of its resting place, swept off the cobwebs and dead leaves, and had a good look at it. It was wooden, with small eight-inch wheels, and was framed in with two-foot sides and a four-foot meshed metal back that could be dropped down for loading. The sides were attached to the front and back with hooks that just dropped into O ring–style screws. Not exactly the safest set up, but I had been too cheap to replace them with more secure fittings and I'd had no problems in the past. That trailer had been used to haul furniture and even a motorcycle on occasion, so I figured it could handle a refrigerator just fine. So what if the tires were bald, cracking, and flat? I filled up the tires and towed the trailer around the neighborhood for a while to loosen up its stiff joints. It creaked, moaned, and whined as it moved along. People turned their heads to see what was causing the noise, but I really didn't care as it was only coming out of retirement for a short period of time. I grabbed some rope and old blankets, and off I went.

The seller took a step back when he saw my trailer, but he reluctantly helped me load on the fridge. We pushed it to the front of the trailer, covered it with the blankets, and then basically wedged it in the right corner so that it rested against the front and side panels of the trailer. We wrapped the rope around it so many times that it looked like a spider web making camp. The rope crisscrossed and overlapped until it was used up. There was no way that fridge was going to move even one iota.

I took it slow and easy on the way home, using only back roads, to avoid drawing any attention. All was going well until I saw a large pothole in front of me. I swerved to miss it and did, but was not so lucky with the trailer. The passenger side trailer wheel disappeared into this canyon. There was a loud bang as the tire blew up. The trailer immediately leaned way over to the right and the fridge pressed heavily on the side panel. The panel buckled like a wet noodle and fell right off and onto the road. I don't know how it happened, but for some reason the lower part of the fridge stayed in the trailer while the top half tilted over until it hit the sidewalk and started dragging on it. There were sparks flying everywhere. The fridge scraped along the sidewalk, bouncing up and down, gouging and slicing the sidewalk. By the time I got the car stopped, the fridge had left a thirty-foot path of destruction. It was awful! It looked like a jackhammer had run amok.

There was quite a large crowd by the time the police arrived. The officer shook his head in disbelief that someone could actually be stupid enough to undertake such a risky venture, let alone use a trailer that was on life support. After he wrote me the first ticket for driving with a poorly secured load, he flipped over the page and wrote me a second ticket. This ticket was basically for indecent exposure of a trailer. Hauling this piece of trash on a public road was an offense. He then left. I think the crowd thought he had been a little harsh on me.

It was only a short time afterward that a public works truck pulled up behind me, with his trailer in tow. He and his buddy loaded the crushed fridge onto their trailer. He then got out two large, bright yellow caution barricades and placed them at each end of the ruined sidewalk. I had to agree that the sidewalk looked really bad and was not fit to be walked on. Before he closed his door and took off, he made me aware that there would be a charge for them to take the fridge to the dump. He did casually mention as well that the taxpayers

## The Cheap Handyman

would not be the ones footing the bill for the replacement of the sidewalk. I prided myself on having a good insurance policy but, regrettably, I think stupidity was excluded from coverage.

**Estimated cost of fridge pickup:** $0

**Actual cost of fridge pickup:** $2,700

## Episode 31

### DUCKLING AROUND

I can be a man of mercy when it comes to animals, even little ducklings. I recall many years ago when a pheasant accidently smashed into the glass of our patio door. The bang was so loud that I slopped hot coffee down the front of me. He obviously didn't see it but did hurt himself in the process. I remember I ran out and saw him lying there. I grabbed a box to put him in and rushed him to a nearby vet. He had a broken wing, so I left him in the vet's care. Without telling anyone, I visited the injured guy every day to see how he was doing. The vet said that our little friend would be able to go to the animal shelter before too long and would then be released back into the wild at the appropriate time.

Anyway, each year, like clockwork, these same two ducks arrive and take root in our pool, as soon as the cover is taken off in the spring. I'm convinced they come from Florida. They lock their radar in on our place, pack a small bag, and head off to their summer vacation destination. We try to shush them away as we know they see our pool as a copulating haven, but we can never encourage them to go elsewhere. They do disappear for a short while but then seem to return in the dead of night and do what they do best while we are sleeping, because every year we wake up and there's a herd of baby ducklings swimming in the pool. This year there were twelve of them, plus mom and dad.

I must admit I enjoyed watching the cute little things swimming around. They scoot from one point to another like little missiles and then abruptly do a deep dive. One goes, then another, and then another. It's one of those funny things you could sit around and watch for hours. But something a little different happened this year. The water level was lower than normal, and I saw that they could not get out of the pool by means of the steps on their own. Even though they were great little swimmers, they would have to rest at some point. I went into panic mode!

I did, of course, first think of raising the water level, but it would have taken hours for the water to rise even a few inches. That could have resulted in fatalities, and I wasn't going to take that chance. So, the first thing I did was to grab a pool noodle, hoping that one at a time they would waddle up the blue foam to safe ground, but each time I approached one a submarine dive took place. By now I had the parents on each side of me, about five feet away, squawking expectantly at top volume as if this were all my fault. I could feel myself breaking into a sweat! I ran to my shed and grabbed a four-by-eight piece of plywood and placed it in the shallow end of the pool by the steps. The ducklings could use it like a ramp to walk out of the water and onto the cement. I watched carefully as some of them ventured toward the plywood, but they would only go to the edge of the water. They were so close! Instinctively I stepped onto the board, reached out as far as I could to help them, and then proceeded to lose my footing and fall face-first right onto the plywood. My nose broke my fall and started bleeding profusely. To make things worse, the wood started to slide down from my weight, and I could hear the liner tearing beside me. What a mess! I was now partially in the pool and wet, so on my hands and knees I slowly climbed out, grabbed a towel for my nose, and looked at the damage in disgust. I was still on a mission to get the ducks out. No one was going to drown on my watch!

My last-resort rescue procedure was using the net we used to scoop out leaves. I was not at all comfortable with doing this, but unless I did something very soon there would be fatalities. Slowly, like a snake in the grass, I snuck up on each duckling one by one and carefully scooped it out and placed it softly on the cement. It seemed like it was taking forever to get the twelve boys and girls out until I realized that each one, once on the cement, ran behind me and jumped back into the water. They thought this was a great game. I then started the process again and lifted each survivor over the fence and onto the grass where dad quickly escorted it to a safer place. It took some time, but the mission was successful with no casualties.

We covered up the pool until further notice. We watched

## The Cheap Handyman

for the return of our little friends but did not see them again.
However, we did hear some squawking a few days later from
our neighbors a few doors down. They had a bigger pool than
us and the ducks were obviously settling in just fine.

Estimated cost of rescue: $0

Actual cost of rescue: $300

*Episode 32*

## LOSING MY BEARINGS

I really enjoy riding my bicycle. When I lost my other bike on the camping trip, I quickly replaced it and had already ridden this one a great deal. We were fortunate enough to live in an area with country roads and beautiful hilly, scenic terrain. I always felt free when I was on it, without a care in the world. I'd jump on my mountain bike at least once a day and just cruise around the neighborhood for hours. It was great therapy for me. It consistently rode smoothly and quietly and allowed me to think about things on my mind and how to resolve them. It was heavenly. On this particular ride everything was great, until I started to hear a grinding sound from the front wheel. It was annoying and disrupting my peace. I'd have to do something about this!

The local bike repair shop guy was very helpful. He quickly diagnosed the problem to be bad bearings. He was an honest fellow and I appreciated that. He suggested that I purchase new bearings and install them myself. He stated that he'd be glad to do the repair but couldn't get to it for at least three weeks. He said it was so easy, and that all I'd have to do was go online and watch a video for this kind of repair. I purchased the bearings and headed home, pumped to get started.

I watched the video on YouTube he'd recommended, and it seemed that the process was straightforward. Basically, it was three steps: take the wheel off the bike, remove the bad bearings, replace them with the new ones. Done. It was so simple that it seemed any moron could accomplish this task. In the garage, with the necessary tools beside me, I flipped the bike upside down and lifted the front wheel out of the forks. I spotted the bearings immediately. The metal balls were in a circular cone, compressed with a cup with curved walls located in the wheel hub. The instructions emphasized that the worn bearings may take some work to get out and could possibly put up quite a fight. The video clearly stated that the new bearings should slide in easily and without a trace of friction. In my case the old bearings did need some persuasion to come out, but I struggled with the new ones. In fact, I had no choice but to grab The Beast to tap them in. Nonetheless, they were finally in place. Very pleased with myself that the job was done and in short order, I reattached the front wheel and turned the bike right side up. Time for a test drive!

I jumped on my machine and took off. The bike ran like a champ. It was so smooth and quiet that I thought I was riding a Swiss watch. Man did it feel good! As I headed for the first hill, I accelerated a bit to make sure that I'd make it to the top. Once there, I stopped for a minute before heading down. With my foot on the pedal I began the descent.

The bike cruised flawlessly at first, picking up speed until halfway down the hill. I heard a familiar sound. That noisy grinding was back, and worse than before. The wheel started to wobble and seize up. Out of control, my bike veered to the right and directed me toward the top of a hill with a steep, scary slope. I started the plummet, bouncing and banging my way down. I slammed on the brakes, but their effect was minimal. I felt like a balloon where someone had undone the end and it was spurting air out in all directions. I weaved through brush and trees, dodging the small bushes scattered everywhere and ducking under whip-like tree branches for survival. I somehow managed to miss hitting these body-busting obstacles and ended up coasting parallel to the stream at the bottom of the hill. The front wheel locked up and the bike collapsed, dumping me into the stream and injuring my wrist along with my pride.

I crawled out of the water and ventured over to the clump on the ground. As expected, the bike now looked like a pretzel. The wheel was bent in every direction possible. The forks would never see the light of day again. I mounted it over my shoulders like I had someone in the fireman's lift and headed up the hill. It was shocking how long I had to wait for some passerby to stop and help me. I almost had to lie in the middle of the road to get some attention.

I took my crumpled wheel back to the bike shop. The poor thing was so mangled that there was nothing to be done. Still, I had to know what went wrong! I had paid great attention to the video and was proud of myself for not taking any short-

**The Cheap Handyman**

cuts in following the instructions, which, I have to admit, I had done many times in the past. In this case I followed them to the letter. In a glance the bike shop worker stated that I had installed the bearings backward. He was sly as he hinted that even the dimmest of the dimmest should not have made that mistake. The next day, wrist bandaged, I gazed melancholically out my front window at my best bud, my bike, now a tangled wreck lying there with the rest of the garbage, waiting to be picked up. The cost of repairs would be too much. It seemed the right time to move on and buy another bike, again. I will miss you!

Estimated cost of repairs: $65

Actual cost of repairs: $495

*Episode 33*

## NEVER SAW IT COMING

I always knew I was a little on the cheap side. My friends reminded me of this on a regular basis and there were plenty of duct tape repair jobs around my home to serve as proof. I was no different when it came to outside activities. Like tennis lessons. I had always wanted to learn to play. I regularly watched the tournaments on TV and was so impressed by their play. It inspired me to take some lessons. These pros made the game look so easy. It always amazed me how they could hit the ball so hard and always know where it was going, serve the ball at one hundred miles plus per hour and hit the target most of the time—that was a real talent! I had made some inquiries into the cost of private lessons and was astounded at what they charged for a one-hour lesson. The receptionist at the tennis club threw out the idea of renting a ball machine. Come out and hit a few balls first, see if you have a feel for the game, and then decide on whether or not you want to take lessons. It was relatively inexpensive to rent, and, me being me, I went for the machine.

I arrived at the tennis club with my brand-new can of tennis balls in my bag looking like a real rookie. I had just purchased shorts, a top, shoes, socks, sweatband, and a racket. I was ready to go. One of the instructors was kind enough to set up the ball machine for me and give me a quick rundown on how it worked. He cautioned me on correctly setting the speed at which the balls left the machine, as they could fire out up to one hundred miles per hour. I thanked him for his help, and he left.

Anxious to start hitting the ball, I set the speed at thirty miles per hour and stood at the baseline. The machine was at the other baseline. I used the remote control to angle the delivery of the balls. They bounced nicely in front of me and allowed me to hit them easily. There was nothing to this game. I danced around from my forehand to my backhand like a ballerina on a dance floor. I soon adjusted the speed up to fifty, then seventy, then ninety miles per hour. I was having a blast trying to return these rockets. For a change of pace, I thought I'd try my luck volleying at the net. I'd watched the professionals do it, and it looked like a lot of fun. I took my "ready" position stance about two feet from the net, put my racket in front of me, adjusted my glasses, bent my knees a little, and then hit the fire button on the remote. The ball came out fast, hit me directly between the eyes, broke my glasses sending pieces flying in all directions, and leveled me flat on my back. I never even saw it coming. It knocked me out cold! I came to a few minutes later sprawled out on the court with a paramedic looking over me. A couple of people standing around thought I was dead. I was checked over, and aside from the little stream of blood running down from the point of impact,

I was okay; I was encouraged to lie there for a while. I did and then quickly gathered my stuff and got the hell out of there. Once again, I was mortified. My aspirations of becoming a tennis star were shot. I'd never be able to show my face in that tennis club again on the off chance someone might remember the goof who just about killed himself. At home I laid low. My wife asked how I got the cut on the bridge of my nose. I reluctantly told her my story. Her response was predictable. The shake of her head from side to side followed by the head drop and walk away was all too familiar to me.

The next day I went to have my eyes checked after being bashed in the face. Fortunately, everything was fine. I then took my broken glasses to the optician. They looked like road-kill and were pronounced dead on arrival. There was no hope of fixing these. For a mere $700 my expensive-framed, prescription glasses were replaced.

**Estimated cost of tennis: $15 0**

**Actual cost of tennis: $85 0**

*Episode 34*

## A COOL POOL

I was grateful to have a heater to keep the water in my pool a comfortable ninety degrees. My wife in particular wouldn't put a toe in it if the temperature dropped even a degree below that. When I got the first heating bill, I did a double take. I thought for sure there was a mistake and got into a verbal fisticuff with the guy on the other end of the phone. I was hopping mad and asked him if I sounded like someone who was stupid, and he responded by saying nothing. He was right, though. He explained the reason for the high bill, and sadly it made sense. I said to my wife that I hoped she was in the pool at least ten hours a day, to offset the enormous cost of keeping it heated. It was a luxury to have a heated pool, though. We could jump in it anytime we wanted. If the weather cooled off, the pool temperature would never be affected. We really enjoyed jumping into the warm water, even at midnight. It was kind of cool to be able to do that.

But this particular heater was the most useless piece of crap ever invented. Each year when I opened the pool the serviceman would have to come, and I'd have to dish out $200 for the twenty minutes it took him to get it going. Spiders, he said, plugging up the system. After about six years of this nonsense, I'd had enough. The last time he came I watched closely as his fingers danced around the inside parts of the heater. The next time this happened, and it would, I'd fix the problem myself.

Next year swung around and, right on cue, the heater wouldn't cooperate once again. I turned the gas off, took off the front panel as the serviceman had, and stared thoughtfully at the inside of the unit, trying to remember what the serviceman had done. I couldn't see any spiders, spider webs, spider eggs, spider dung, spider footprints, or for that matter anything to do with spiders. Nonetheless, flying blind, I started to remove parts carefully. I kept removing parts, looking for clues, until I realized that I'd removed upwards of twenty parts. There were more pieces of hardware spread out around me on the patio than were left in the heater. I didn't remember him removing nearly as many items. Baffled, I took a few steps back to review the situation. It wasn't until I heard the first crunch that I realized I had stepped on and flattened about half a dozen key components of the heater that I'd placed on the ground directly behind me. The pieces resembled the dregs of a bag of potato chips. Any prudent individual with even a hint of common sense would have known enough to place the removed parts in a safe area. I looked at the wreckage and cringed. Some of the parts looked complex and very expensive. In a panic I got out my tools and tried to fix some of the damaged goods. I tried to twist the pilot assembly back into shape but with no luck. I grabbed my loyal

## The Cheap Handyman

graphite hammer, The Beast, and tried hammering the crap out of the heat exchanger hoping to restore it back into useable form. I had no luck in restoring any of the parts I stepped on. Nothing worked! I went online to see if I could buy the replacement parts myself, but I didn't know the names of them, let alone how to find them. In the end, stupidity reigned supreme and I realized that replacement parts purchased from the heater company and professionally installed was the only restitution. I'd have to call in the cavalry. I was pissed! My hands were shaking as I headed for the phone.

It was about three weeks before the serviceman returned. During that time, I had to endure the silent treatment from the family as they swam in an unheated pool. The serviceman seemed to have an extra bounce in his step when he arrived. I sweated it out as he sang while he worked, tossing out the old parts and unpacking shiny, new, expensive-looking parts from their boxes. About two hours later he was finished and graciously handed me the bill. I was stunned! I could have bought a new heater for this. Never again would I put my hands on something this far out of my depth.

**Estimated cost of job:** $0

**Actual cost of job:** $850

*Episode 35*

## IT'LL ALL COME OUT
## IN THE WASH

All the banging and clanging from our washing machine was really starting to get to me. It shook so much that the living room floor vibrated like one of those ten-cent vibrating beds in a cheap hotel. When that rocket fired up, we instinctively grabbed our drinks from the table or they would have been shaken right off it. It was one of those old, heavy-duty, built-like-a-tank machines that probably spent a great deal of its life in a laundromat somewhere. When the load was finished it blurted out a loud, disturbing honk that would lift us off our seats. To top it off, the ol' clunker was leaking water onto the floor. The cost of having a service person come out was more than what the machine was worth, so I'd do the leg work myself. It was at least worth my time to try and fix this baby. If all else failed, we'd be pounding the pavement looking for a new one. My mission statement today, however, was to fix the water leak. I was quite sure that the O ring in the agitator was the cause of the ruckus. My bet was it had dried out and cracked. All I needed to do was replace it.

Turns out that was easier said than done. Our washer was a top-loading machine. I'd have to stick half my body into it in order to fix it. It was all too easy to envision getting stuck in there and having the firemen use the jaws of life to slice open the washer to get me out. In order to investigate the root of the problem, I'd have to remove a few parts first. I lifted the lid, and looking down into the hollow of the agitator I could see the fabric softening dispenser sitting on top of the agitator. It pulled right off without a hitch. Next to come off was the agitator cap, which was about five inches inside the hollow. I had to insert a flathead screwdriver along the edge of the agitator cap and agitator, twist the screwdriver, and pop off the cap of the agitator. I also used needle-nose pliers to assist in the process. Sometimes these caps could be really stuck in there and could break when trying to get them out. It always made my day when that happened. In my case, I was lucky, and the cap came out intact. I was on a roll! I then connected a socket extension to my socket wrench and went to town to remove the agitator bolt from inside the agitator, which held the agitator in place. Taking out that bolt was like wrestling with a pit bull. The more I twisted, the more it seemed to twist back. I was bent over and grunting, groaning, sweating, swearing, and farting trying to get that damn bolt to move. It was truly a test of my patience. Eventually it gave way, and I unscrewed it and pulled out the agitator. The third part just pulled right up and off. Peering down into the washer I could see the remaining mechanics of the agitator and the tiny, thin O ring way down there.

What none of the videos told me was that from this point on you needed the small hands of a five-year-old to reach it. Poking around with my screwdriver, I finally got the O ring off. It was no surprise to see that it was dried out. I called the manufacturer to order a new O ring, which cost about ninety cents, but was informed that one could not buy *just* the O ring. I had hoped to fast track things here by describing the O ring to him over the phone, and if it had some markings on it, he could easily look it up and let me know if he had any in stock. He stated that I had to buy the entire agitator unit, which came with its own O ring. He said he could sell me a refurbished unit for $250. I told him that this was highway robbery, but he didn't really care. I hung up in a hissy fit. I'd simply track down my own O ring from a local store. With the original ring in my hand, I went from store to store, showed the salespeople the old ring, and hoped that someone would have an identical spare. Even knowing the make and model of the washer, sadly no one had an exact match. The machine was just too old. I had to settle for one as close to the original as possible. To err on the side of caution, I bought three of them.

Putting the unit back together was just about as difficult as taking it apart. I had to have Superman's vision to even see where the O ring went. I grabbed my most powerful flashlight and shone it down the hole of the agitator. With two fingers I started to slide the O ring down from the top and toward its resting place. The ring slipped off my fingers and fell somewhere into the agitator mechanism. I never did find it. I almost had the second ring on when it snapped in half. By now I was close to losing it. With slow and careful deliberation, I finally slide the last O ring into its proper spot. It slid on a bit too easily for my liking, and I worried that it should fit more snugly, but that replacement ring was the only game in town and would have to do. With everything locked back into place, I started up the washer and laid on the floor beside it looking hawkishly beneath the unit for leaks. After ten minutes I saw none and was confident that this old clunker still had some miles left in her. I considered this another job completed.

We had to run a few errands later that day, and we put a load in the washer before we left. Upon our arrival back home, something didn't seem kosher. Before we even got to the living room, we could hear the whooshing of water, and rounding the corner, which was right beside the laundry room, we stopped short in horror. Our living room was on a slightly lower level than the laundry room and was now filled with about three inches of water. It looked like a swimming pool for toddlers. I ran for my rubber boots and waded through the room to the washing machine. It was spewing water from somewhere. I prayed it was something as simple as one of the black rubber water lines breaking and not something I had done. I turned the washer off, tilted it back as far as it would go, and dunked my head sideways into the small amount of water on the floor to get a look underneath. Most of it had flowed into the living room. Three cheers for old houses with uneven floors. I could still see a steady flow of water oozing out from the base of the agitator. Clearly, I had made a poor choice of O rings. As I had feared, it was too loose. I should have known better, and for that I'd paid a price. I should never have settled for second best. I felt like pounding my head against the wall a few times.

I was lucky that a friend of mine owned a restoration company. He could have a crew to my place within a few hours. They arrived with their huge shop vacs and fans the size of refrigerators and within hours they had the water sucked up, the soaked carpet removed, and the floor dry. The couch, chairs, and tables were also wet and were just tossed in the backyard for now. To avoid the risk of mold going up the walls, they also cut away about twelve inches of drywall from the floor up throughout the entire room. I was impressed with their work, but I suspected I wouldn't be impressed with what would follow in the mail. Friend or not, an invoice was imminent. This ordeal was going to be a big kick in the fanny. The whole thing was a total "wash." From the get-go my gut told me that a makeshift O ring was a bad idea, but I did it anyway. *Just buy the damn refurbished unit and get on with it*, is what I should have told myself.

From this point on I was going to tape a note to the wall beside whatever task I was about to undertake. It would say,

### The Cheap Handyman

"Gut to human, do you know what you're doing?" Now, the entire living room would be getting a face-lift, not to mention our ol' washer.

Estimated cost of job: $1.29

Actual cost of job: $2,800

*Episode 36*

**DOING A GOOD DEED**

**FOR A CREATURE IN NEED**

I have to admit that I hate mice. They are a downright nuisance. Even though you never know how, sometimes they manage to slip into the house, eat crumbs of food left around the place, and even nibble furniture to the point that it has to be replaced. They are anything but clean. These small rodents are a pest and like to invade homes. My personal favorite is seeing their pellet-like droppings scattered everywhere. I always feared that some night I'd wake up and see one of those critters sitting on my chest, staring at me. But when I see a baby mouse stranded on the plastic hook inside the pool, even I have to show some compassion. He was sitting there on his little back legs, perched up and shaking, scared to death. I didn't know how he got there, but I had to do something. I'd perform a rescue.

Looking around for something long enough to serve as a bridge, my eyes fell on a pool noodle. I carefully positioned it so that I held one end in my hand with the other end just touching the hook. To my surprise the little critter bolted up the noodle and then straight up my arm. He scared the crap out of me! Reflexively, I flung my arm up into the air and cata-pulted the mouse into space, so high that I lost sight of him for a moment. I was so startled that I fell backward right into our beautiful, expensive, plastic, never-to-rust fence that sur-rounded the pool. I flattened the gate like a pancake along with a huge section on each side of the gate. Looking from my ground position I could see that numerous other sections were badly twisted. I was speechless.

Regaining my composure, I thought I'd better search for my astronaut. Sadly, my search and rescue mission failed, and it turned into a search and recover mission. I would have felt better if I could have found even some body parts so that I could bury him with dignity, but I realized that he flew so high up into the air that the impact alone hitting the ground prob-ably scattered him all over the backyard. I couldn't even find a mouse hair. This was truly a sad time for me.

I wish I could say that my only thoughts were for the mouse, but seeing that fence made my heart fall into my stomach. It was a mess, all twisted and bent and helplessly lying on its side. I thought I could hear it whimpering a bit. Most things I try to fix myself, but this repair job was well above my pay grade. I'd have to call in the experts.

They could do the work, they told me, but not for about three weeks. Being kind of an emergency situation, I knew it was not going to be cheap. As it was a pool fence, I couldn't leave the pool area unprotected, so I had to purchase a tem-porary fence. Of course, no hardware stores had any suitable

B.S. Harris

fencing in stock, so for a mere $300 I picked up a make-do, disposable fence from a pool company. So much for trying to save a creature in need!

**Estimated cost of rescue:** $0

**Actual cost of rescue:** $750

*Episode 37*

## RAINDROPS KEEP FALLING
## ON MY HEAD

At the far end of our backyard we had a rather large shed that I converted into a rec room for the kids. Over time I had added heating and lighting, not to mention installing a window air conditioner, so that it pretty much had all the comforts of home, I thought. Not too long after the kids starting using it they came to me and stated that as much as they appreciated all the work I'd done in the shed, it was still lacking one thing: a TV with better reception. The rabbit ears I had dug up from downstairs simply weren't cutting it. Kids need to be able to watch more than four stations these days. Much as I wanted to, I couldn't really disagree with them—what's a clubhouse without a TV with at least thirty stations on it? I'd have to run a TV cable line from the house to the shed. The quotes from the professionals were, as usual, completely outrageous, so I'd do it myself. An average guy like me should be able to pull this off without hardly breaking a sweat.

I rented a "digger," as I called it, which looked much like an overgrown jigsaw. It basically had a giant jigsaw blade at the bottom which gyrated and cut a narrow, eight-inch-deep trench in the grass, which I was told was the depth needed to run the cable line. There were two models of the machine available, one being self-propelled and one not. As I didn't want to lay out the extra cash for the self-propelled unit, I opted for the basic one. I also purchased the one hundred feet of cable needed and was ready to start.

It didn't take long to realize that I should have rented the deluxe model. This monster was extremely heavy and a lung buster. I sweated every inch I pushed that bad boy, but I was making progress. About ten feet in I ran into some resistance and thought I'd hit a rock, so I applied a little extra muscle and ploughed ahead. It ran smoothly again, but then I was stopped. More flex, and then it was clear sailing right up to the shed. I drilled a hole in the low corner of the structure, ran the cable through, and hooked it up to the TV. The other end of the cable easily attached to an available junction point inside the cable box. A quick test showed that the TV worked magnificently. The kids now had a lot more stations to choose from. Another job well done!

Later that night my wife and I were sleeping in bed when we heard rainfall hitting the roof. Strange, since there had been a beautiful sunset which normally implied no rain, and there wasn't any in the forecast. I got up and looked out the window. There were what looked like two gushers similar to what you'd see if an oil rig ran amok, but in this case, it was water shooting fifteen feet into the air. I had no idea what was going on, so I headed out to the backyard. I got soaked as I stepped outside. I stared at this phenomenon, and it suddenly hit me as to what had happened. Those two bumps in

## The Cheap Handyman

the road when I cut the trench weren't rocks. I must have cut through the sprinkler system line. Twice! And now the system was in pieces. The way the water was shooting straight up told me that I must have nicked the top part of the sprinkler line, ripping a hole in it. The strong water pressure took care of the rest. I was instantly pissed. It was set to come on every third night, and now instead of watering the entire lawn it was shooting up to the stars. That sprinkler system was only put in last year and not cheap. The warranty would not cover stupidity. I turned off the control panel and would deal with it in the morning.

The sprinkler guy was gracious when I called. He said he'd been in business more than twenty years and had never heard of anyone slicing up the sprinkler line in that fashion. Yup, that made me feel so much better. The waiting time for his arrival was more than two weeks, and by then the grass looked like straw. I'm glad there weren't any cows or horses in the neighborhood, as they could have had a few good meals on us. I watched painfully as the repairman spent hours cutting out about fifteen feet of lawn and then the sprinkler line and replacing it. I could only hope he'd water down the bill he'd be sending me.

**Estimated cost of job: $120**

**Actual cost of job: $360**

## *Episode 38*

## RUNAWAY SHINGLES

It was that time again for the roof to be replaced. It seemed like only yesterday that I was up there pulling shingles off my roof, even though almost twenty years had passed since then. Last time I had the professionals do it and it cost me an arm and a leg; this time, my buddies and I were doing it. A few years ago, when a friend needed a new roof, we all pitched in and helped him. It had now become a tradition to step up when necessary. We fancied ourselves the weekend warrior roofers. One of the guys was a contractor who acted as the supervisor to make sure us misfits didn't screw up, and so far we had done half a dozen roofs together.

All I had to do was order the materials and have them delivered the day before my crew showed up. I ordered the shingles, nails, etc., as well a few pieces of plywood, just in case some of it had to be replaced. The truck arrived right on time, and with their fancy lift machine they raised the shingles, a skid at a time, up to the roof. A couple of guys then stacked the bundles of shingles on the crest of the roof. These guys looked like they were twelve years old and new to the job. I questioned them on how they were stacking large bundles on top of each other creating a very heavy load on the roof. They said this was how it was done and that it wasn't their first rodeo.

I had a larger than normal lump in my throat as I looked up at the four humungous stacks of shingles on the peak. My gut told me that this was an accident looking for a place to happen. All I needed was for my roof to cave in from the weight of the load. I felt sick just thinking about the damage that would do. I most certainly could not let those stacks of shingles stay where they were. I remembered from one of our other roofing jobs being told to spread out the shingles when loading a pickup, as too heavy a load in one spot could damage the shocks of the vehicle. It seemed like the same applied here, so I decided I would spread out the bundles, as a cautionary measure.

To help the guys out, I'd stack the bundles in groups of five and scatter them all over the roof. This would substantially reduce the load that was on the peak of the roof and would also save time for the lackeys doing all the grunt work. Man, were those bundles heavy! It was like dragging around dead bodies. I was a little concerned about stacking the bundles five high without some kind of support around them as the roof did have some slope to it. It was only going to be one night, though—what could go wrong between now and tomorrow morning?

I was really tired that night as I hit the sack. I thought it was a very smart thing I'd done in sorting out the bundles. Just lying there peacefully, I heard this noise. I couldn't put my finger on it. It sounded like someone was dragging something. Then suddenly I heard a loud bang, and then three more bangs after that. I jumped up and listened. I didn't hear anything else, so I laid back down. Tomorrow some poor bugger would find something wrong. Not my problem!

The next morning brought with it a sunny day. A perfect day to get the roof replaced. I was feeling good as I walked out the front door and awaited the arrival of my buddies. Stepping onto the driveway, I glanced to the right and then just about dropped dead. On top of the roof of my wife's car were four bundles of shingles. They were so heavy that they caved in the entire roof, bending it down so much that the inside ceiling liner was hanging over the headrest. My wife's Ford was a small car to start with, but it looked a lot smaller now. The dragging noise I heard last night must have been the bundles of shingles sliding one by one off the roof, flying through the air, and landing on the car. It was clear to me now that I should never have stacked the bundles five high without some sort of support. At some point gravity kicked in and each bundle directly above the parked car? Once again, I had outdone myself. This time it was worse than ever: I was well used to the jabs and raised eyebrows of my family, but my friends? Another story that would probably outlive me. Nonetheless, without further incident, two days later we completed laying the shingles. Never a better roof had anyone ever seen!

# The Cheap Handyman

I was getting quite used to visiting my body shop man. In all my previous encounters I was able to drive my vehicles to his shop. This time my vehicle arrived, ungraciously, on the back of a tow truck. It was so badly damaged that I couldn't even get into the driver's seat. He could hardly wait to hear what happened this time.

Estimated cost of roof:  $2,200

Actual cost of roof:  $4,900

*Episode 39*

I had a mountain bike that I really liked. Over the years, bending over to reach the handlebars has taken its toll on my body. Aside from giving me an aching back, bent and twisted shoulders, and numbness in both hands, the bike was fine. However, I couldn't continue like that. It was either buy a new bike or come up with a solution for my bike. I wasn't going to spend the money on a new bike, so I decided I would put on a handlebar extension stem. It would raise the handlebars about three inches, which would hopefully take away some of those aches. To avoid getting myself in trouble from the get-go, I went online to see how much a stem was and how complicated it would be to install it myself. The price to purchase it was reasonable. I thought I'd check into the cost of someone else installing it. I had a bike shop within walking distance from me that was run by two really nice guys. They said they wouldn't pay to have it installed if they were me, as it was so simple even a baby could do it. That was good enough for me. I'd track down an extension stem.

Online there were dozens of them available. I ended up choosing the one that was most popular and had the least complicated instructions. It arrived within a few days, and I was ready to go. There were only four instructions, with each one having about ten words. So, with only forty words of instruction in total, I could see where the guys said that even a baby could successfully complete this task. I brought my bike to the center of the garage floor where it would be easy to work. I read the instructions for the third time and began. To do this job I only needed an Allen wrench. Using it, I removed the long bolt from the clamping tube that held the handlebars in place. I pulled the handlebars up and out and delicately placed them on the front wheel of the bike. My next step was to put the extension bar in the tube, put the handlebars into it, then replace and tighten the bolt, and we were done. Before doing this, I decided to move the bike to a more brightly lit part of the garage so I could see more clearly. I lifted the bike up, and immediately the front forks fell out of the frame and hit the cement floor. In a second, the fork bearings bounced right out of their holder and scattered in all directions; the handlebars were thrown to one side, bending and ripping the brake line close to the right brake handle. I was so disgusted that I just dropped the entire bike. I remembered the comment about a baby. In reality, nothing would rattle my cage more than poor instructions. There was no mention about securing the forks so that they wouldn't plummet to the ground.

I could see bearings all over the floor. There were supposed to be twenty in total. Five were still in the harness but the others were everywhere. I picked up the ones just lying there in plain sight and moved all kinds of junk around in the garage looking for the others. I found a few more, but there were still a lot missing that seemed to have just vanished. After about half an hour I gave up. I was about to snap. I knew the bearings were a lost cause now, so I focused my efforts on the broken brake line. In some cases the brake line can just detach itself from the brake handle. If this happens, it is a quick, easy fix. You just push the brake lever right up to the bar, slide the cable back into the hole, push it through the slit in the brake, and tighten the locking mechanism. I'd done it many times before. In my case though, the brake line bent and snapped about eight inches from the handle, which meant the entire line would have to be replaced. It was a double defeat for me. I was beyond words by now.

I grabbed a plastic bag and threw the bearings in it along with a few other assorted parts that had fallen off the bike. I threw the bag and bike into my vehicle and shamefully headed off to the bike shop. The guys stood there nonresponsive when I told them what happened. A job that required only one tool was almost unheard of these days. To only have to remove one part, put a second part under the first part, and replace the first part was a gift. It couldn't be any simpler than that, yet for some of us it was a challenge of a grand proportion.

**Estimated cost of job:** $30

**Actual cost of job:** $190

## Episode 40

It was a sad and happy time for us. We had recently purchased another home and were now going through the process of selling our cedar home in which we lived for more than thirty years. The kids were grown-up and gone, and the house was more than we needed anymore. We were hoping that a younger couple with kids would buy it—the thought of that gorgeous in-ground pool going to waste was more than I could bear. We were delighted when we heard that our wish had come true. The new owners had three kids all under the age of twelve and a sheltie pup. They could hardly wait to move in.

Most new home buyers insist on having a home inspection done. It's the only way to confirm the home does not hold any dark secrets that may come back to haunt the new occupants at a later time. I had no problem with an inspection as I had worked my fingers to the bone for years to keep that place in tip-top condition. Most inspections are done within an hour or so, but this fellow blasted away for four hours and was extremely thorough. We were not allowed to be there when he carried out his inspection but were relieved to hear

163

that he found nothing wrong except for the disaster in the crawl space under the house. Since I only visited it when I had to turn the water on and off, I hadn't bothered to clean it up. The owners before us had used it as a dumping ground. There were broken cement blocks, bricks, pieces of wood, wires galore, broken windows, and so much more. The only thing not under there, to my knowledge, was a dead body.

The biggest eyesore, however, was the insulation between the floor joists. It was there to keep the floor of the living room and kitchen above it warm, which it hadn't done. Most of it was just hanging from the joists and doing nothing other than looking ugly. It was a hell of a mess to look at and an even worse one to clean up. Our house was sold on the condition that the old insulation would be removed and replaced with new insulation. It was a job I wouldn't wish on my worst enemy. A few quick calls for quotes confirmed that I'd be doing this myself.

We were fortunate that the old insulation was not the asbestos kind that could cause serious health concerns. Ours was fiberglass insulation, which we could remove and dispose of ourselves. To be on the safe side I did pick up a few things to make the job easier, including a respirator, heavy-duty gloves, well-fitting safety glasses, a hazmat suit, rubber boots, a box of plastic trash bags, and a cushion to lie on as my butt was going to get mighty sore.

I just about gagged as I laid on my back and started hauling the stuff down. It was a tedious, piss-you-off job. I bagged it and then put it into a second bag for added sealing. The long and painful ordeal went on for three days until all the old insulation was out of the house and safely transported to a special waste disposal facility. I remember my final crawl out of that torture chamber. The cheeks of my butt were just screaming and so tight that I could feel them pulsating all night when I slept. I now knew what it was like to have calluses on your ass. I had many libations that night, as I knew that the next day I'd be on my back again, this time putting up new insulation.

The temperature in our neck of the woods never got that cold, so I went with R-12 fiberglass insulation, which seemed perfectly sufficient. If we had normally experienced more extreme temperatures, I would have purchased insulation with a higher R factor. I purchased the bundles of insulation along with a sufficient amount of plastic vapor barrier. I was still really tired from the day before when I started to put up the new stuff. It was such a crap job to do and my heart wasn't in it at all. I just wanted to get it done as quickly as possible and get the hell out of there. The part of the brain that does the thinking was turned off. On my back, I wedged the first piece of insulation up between the floor joists and then moved on to the next one. No sooner did I start on the second one that the first one fell down. I could see it was going to be a cat and mouse game if I didn't do something. I knew the vapor barrier had to go up, so I came up with the bright idea of stapling the plastic to the joists which would hold the insulation in place. It was brilliant! It was one of the best ideas I'd had in years and it worked perfectly. Feeling invigorated, I picked up the pace and completed the task in record time. Two days later, my work was done and it looked great.

The home inspector came back the next day, and the two of us crawled under the house for the final inspection. I was pumped and waiting for his praise on how magnificent a job I had done. He immediately started to chuckle and asked what dumbass had done this. Whoever he was, he had put the vapor barrier on the wrong side of the insulation. The barrier should have been put in first directly against the floor with the insulation then pushed into it afterward. It was totally useless where it was. I was silent for a second and then agreed with him that the guy was clearly the dumbest of dumbasses and that I'd be giving him a piece of my mind. I didn't have the guts to say it was me. The inspector left and said he'd return when this mockery was corrected. I'd never be able to close the house deal without his sign-off. I wasn't going through this nightmare again, so I picked up the phone and started dialing.

All being said, I did have my own private chuckle. I recall saying to my buddy a short time ago when he was laying sod— remember Joe, green side up!

**Estimated cost of job: $400**

**Actual cost of job: $1,800**

**Episode 41:**

## RACCOON MISSION

My wife and I had just moved into our new brick town house. It was the first town house we'd ever purchased, and we were loving it. We had enjoyed our cedar home, but it was aging faster than I was, and the constant repairs were getting the better of me. We had just gone to bed as we were quite tired from unpacking boxes all day long. We were lying there chatting as we drifted off to sleep when we heard a loud thumping above us. We thought it was someone walking around on the roof and obviously up to no good. I jumped up, grabbed the baseball bat I always kept beside the bed, and headed down. I picked up my flashlight as I dashed out the front door. I slowly moved the flashlight from side to side covering every inch of the roof but saw no one there. What I did see though were two beady eyes poking out around the upstairs dormer. I knew that behind those eyes was a small head and huge body of a raccoon. We had a staring match for a few minutes, and then he slithered somewhere out of sight. We had the proverbial raccoon in the attic.

These animals meant no harm. It was the wintertime, and he was just looking for a place to get out of the cold for a while and rest his tired body. I was quite sure that our home was one of many he frequented. However, we didn't want him as a drop-in guest for the rest of our lives. I had heard horror stories of these animals hauling down insulation, dumping load after load everywhere, and basically destroying everything in sight. I didn't want to hurt him, I just wanted him out of the attic. A raccoon can become quite fierce when cornered, so it was not a situation I wanted to put myself in. There was only one thing to do: time to call the experts.

A few days later the raccoon rescuers arrived to find the animal had scratched out a large hole at the side of the dormer and welcomed himself in. The normal procedure was to set up a cage at the mouth of the hole, which they did, and wait for the critter to exit into the cage. A few days later we heard banging and clanging, which told us that our friend was now trapped in the cage. We emphasized that we were animal lovers and that the raccoon was to be safely released into the woods a good distance from our place. Thankfully, this friend didn't seem to be rabid, so the rescuers agreed.

Anyone who has ever experienced such a house guest as ours knows that the attic is usually totaled by the time the guest vacates. In many cases he/she could have lived there for years. I had the rescue crew look in the attic while they were there. As expected, they said it was a wreck. For a paltry $1,500 from my wallet they could restore it to its original state. I didn't think it was beyond my mental capacity, so I decided to do the cleanup and repairs myself.

Raccoon dung is toxic, and I'd been warned multiple

times not go up there with just a smile on my face. To do the job safely I grabbed my hazmat suit, safety glasses, a respirator mask, a pooper scooper, rubber gloves, knee pads, and a spray bottle full of water. To get up to the attic I fetched my ladder, and to navigate in this dark attic I also made ready my extension cord and small table lamp. I, of course, tested out both items to make sure they were working before I entered the attic.

It took me about ten minutes to put on all the crazy gear. It was like gowning up for quarantine. I was sweating already and getting agitated from hardly being able to move. I put the ladder in place and from the top of it carefully slid the attic hatch to one side. It struck me how well-made that hatch was. It was only made out of particleboard, but it fit so snugly into the opening. As an added feature, there was also a strip of foam insulation attached to the perimeter of the hatch, for added snugness. It was also painted the same color as the ceiling, so it blended in well. It would have taken some time to do as good a job as this. Other hatches I had seen fit sloppily into the hole and let all kinds of air escape into the attic. I then heaved all the rest of the stuff into the attic. I plugged in the extension cord and climbed my way up. I stood on the very top of the ladder, as it was a bit short, noting that I'd still have to jump up a distance in order to secure a grip on the inside of the attic opening. The opening was not that large, so I was grateful I wasn't a plump guy who would struggle to squeeze his oversize butt into the small attic crevice.

Finally, with some discomfort, I clambered into the attic,

both elbows scratched and bleeding. It must have been one hundred degrees up there. I strategically placed my lamp on a solid base and turned it on. Nothing happened. The lamp simply didn't work. I made sure that the connection was good and that the bulb was tightly screwed in. All that was fine, but the damn thing still wouldn't turn on. I was pissed! All that work to get up here, and I couldn't even begin the cleanup—it was way too dark to see anything. I'd have to head down and find out what went wrong.

The descent was not pleasant. I felt like I had about one hundred pounds of weight strapped to me as I lumbered my way to the attic entrance. On the way there I put my foot through the attic hatch and busted it in half. I'd haphazardly placed it to close to the opening. I felt I'd just destroyed a van Gogh painting. Something else I'd now have to replace, and more money gone. I shuffled my derriere around and into place for the extraction and forced my way through the opening, propping myself up with my elbows, hoping for a controlled landing. Hanging there like a rag on a clothesline, I frantically swung my body around and fluttered my feet trying to find the top of the ladder. The first thing I found was the ceiling light, which I kicked into pieces. I followed that up with busting and hauling down a shoe rack that had been mounted on the wall. I finally hooked the top of the ladder with my foot and dragged it into position. I dropped my sweat-stained corpse onto it and slithered down to the floor. I was exhausted. I had been to hell and back and achieved absolutely nothing positive.

## The Cheap Handyman

I waited a few days before attempting this mission again. It had shaken me, and I had to regain my confidence. I triple checked everything before going up and had purchased a taller, more suitable ladder—I was taking no chances on this second mountain climb. I was a bit intimidated as I entered the black cave again. This time the light worked, however my worst fears had become a reality. I could see that the insulation lying on the attic floor had been torn to shreds and would have to be replaced. Removing the old stuff and hauling up new stuff would be a big job. I wondered if I had any friends left that might help me. I'd have to think about that. The most unsettling thing I saw was the piles of crap that spanned the length and width of the attic. That raccoon must have had an excessive gorging disorder to leave such huge deposits. I'm surprised we hadn't heard him moaning from all his gluttony. All that being said, and aside from me gagging while scooping up the dung, the cleanup went well. The poop was out of the attic. As far as the insulation, it would soon be out with the old and in with the new. I don't care if he was a wild animal, that raccoon should have been ashamed.

**Estimated cost of job:** $75

**Actual cost of job:** $530

*Episode 42*

UNDER PRESSURE

O ur town house was located in a small private cul-de-sac where everyone took pride in their homes and kept them immaculate. When meeting our neighbors for the first time it didn't take one of them long to tactfully let me know that our vinyl siding was filthy and looked despicable. Feeling very uncomfortable, I immediately picked up the phone and obtained some quotes for cleaning the siding. The three quotes were breathtaking and unacceptable. I'd be better off buying my own pressure washer and doing the work myself.

The next day I had a brand-new machine sitting in my garage. The salesperson had cautioned me that my new gas-powered washer was 2800 PSI and powerful and dangerous in the wrong hands. I was highly encouraged to read the manual carefully before firing up the unit.

There was a lot of vinyl siding and gutters on my place, some of which were two stories up. To reach them I would need to climb my eight-foot ladder. I thought it made sense to work on the second level first. I set up my ladder, fired up the machine, and climbed to the top of the ladder with the washer wand in hand. I adjusted the end nozzle to the soap feature and sprayed the soap onto the siding and gutters. I then waited ten minutes as per the instructions in the manual.

After waiting the allotted time, I climbed back up the ladder and looked at all the other cool nozzle adjustments. They went from delicate to general to maximum to flush. The manual said to start with the general setting first to wash off the soap. If that didn't work, I'd go to the maximum setting, but no higher. The first setting hardly rinsed off any soap, and the second setting didn't do much more. I didn't know what to do now as the soap instructions said to absolutely not let the soap dry because it would create problems. There was only one setting left, that being the flush setting. I couldn't remember what the manual had said about it, and I didn't have time to read it again. There was only one way to find out. I set it to the flush setting and hit the trigger. The water shot out like it was fired from a cannon and looked like a laser beam. It scared the hell out of me. The kickback was so strong that it threw me backward right off the ladder and into the hedges, like the bad guy in a movie that is shot but still keeps firing as he falls backward. As I fell into the hedges, I still had my weapon blazing and firing out a steady stream of water rockets. The beam arced across the sky until it hit my next-door neighbor's roof. Upside down I stared in disbelief as the beam striped off a good number of shingles and unbolted his poorly attached satellite dish.

I was sprawled on my back across the hedges with my head almost touching the ground. My eyes popped out as I watched his shingles gracefully fall from the roof like fluttering snowflakes. The dish slid off the roof and did a pendulum swing from the gutter. I thought I was going to hurl.

Fortunately for a guy who just rocketed off a ladder, only my ego was hurt. I collected myself and headed right over to my neighbor's place to apologize. No point stretching out the inevitable. Like a child who had misbehaved I knocked on the door and shamefully explained my latest disaster. I admired the man for not bopping me in the nose. He calmly stated that he would hand deliver the bill when the repairs were done and would appreciate immediate payment. I nodded.

**Estimated cost of job:** $320

**Actual cost of job:** $1,100

*Episode 43*

## DOOR CRASHER

One of my favorite features about the new place was its attached two-car garage—remote openers included. It was so cool! I'd never had a garage before, and I felt like a kid in a candy shop. The only problem was that when you opened and closed the door, it squeaked and groaned so loudly that you could hear it halfway down the block. This was the first thing I'd have to fix. I chose not to call the garage door guys, as I didn't even want to hear what they'd charge. Besides, it probably just needed a little lubrication. I'd tackle this one myself.

From inside the garage, I opened the door and listened as it made various noises. Like many squeaks, a quick shot of lubricant usually does the trick and the noise is gone. I got up on my ladder and squirted everything from head to toe, basically every moving part I could see. I waited ten minutes and then closed the door. The noise was still there and had escalated to the grating pitch of nails on a chalkboard. It made me wince. There was now a popping sound as well that had just joined the party, and I had no idea where that came from. I expanded my work area and lubricated the torsion springs, hinges, and bearings. I had already sprayed the rollers but did them again anyway. I waited half an hour this time and hit the remote. Nothing had changed. I then hit the open button again and listened more closely than ever. It appeared the noise was being caused by the rollers sliding along the tracks.

The rollers were metal and needed to be lubricated periodically. They had a lot of stress on them. These ones had that *clickity clack* sound when the door went up and down, which indicated to me that they were in need of service. So I doused them with a generous amount of the spray and waited. I watched as they moved back and forth in the tracks. Even though the noise was less, there was still too much noise in my opinion. I did notice that there was some play in the one track, and that the rollers wobbled a bit when sliding back and forth. I concluded that the noise stemmed from there. I grabbed The Beast and worked my way down the right side of the track, gently tapping in the lower part of the track that was angled up to minimize the excess movement. The rollers should now glide smoothly and quietly.

Confident that I'd found the true source of the problem, I pressed the remote, looked up, and waited for pure silence. The door started to raise—so far so good. Halfway into its journey, one of the top rollers on the adjusted track side slowed down and then completely locked. There was no movement whatsoever. However, the rollers on the other track continued to move. The frozen track started to creak and twist along with the door. The garage door opener started smoking and shortly afterward gave up the ghost. The silence was deafening now. I knew I had really screwed up this time. I looked at the twisted metal, saddened that my beautiful new garage door was a deformed and mangled mess. It looked like someone had grabbed a piece of paper and crumpled it up. There was no salvaging this disaster. Once again, I was speechless.

I was so embarrassed by my handiwork that I stapled a couple of tarps over the garage opening. The garage door people would already have a field day with this one. I didn't need my new neighbors to be alarmed knowing that a potentially dangerous guy may be living next door.

**Estimate cost of job:  $0**

**Actual cost of job:  $1,400**

*Episode 44*

SUMP PUMP DUMP

We had been in our new home for about a year now. It was new to us, but in reality it was about twenty years old. It was a brick home and nicer than our previous cedar home, which was so much older and felt like it could have been built by pioneers. The previous owner was an older lady who was lovely but very lax in keeping up with repairs. I had already fixed the refrigerator and dishwasher and had now set my sights on the sump pump in the basement. I had no idea how old it was, but it was grinding and squealing more than ever. I felt its life span was just about over. I had purchased a new pump about a month ago (on sale, naturally), but had deliberately delayed installing it. I really hated doing this kind of work. It was a messy job. When reaching into a sump pump hole to haul out the old pump, I always feared that some unidentifiable bug or slime culture would attach itself to my arm and start feasting. The thought of it made my skin crawl.

I initially considered having someone else put it in, but their quote scared me off. It was a good, strong, one-horse-power pump, so powerful that it would drain water from the hole in a matter of seconds. It was peace of mind that we should not flood, ever. We were due for a huge storm coming the next day, so my time to procrastinate was up: I'd better get my ass in gear and change it right now before we had a problem. I'd had a flooded basement many years ago, and it was a deeply unpleasant situation. I had no sump pump and took in so much water that the furnace and washer and dryer had to be replaced, not to mention having to rent huge vacuums to suck out the water. No insurance coverage was available in that area, so I once again was forced to call on my friends. When I think of it now, I don't really have many friends left. I did not want to go through that again. I was a little hesitant to start the job this very minute as it was ten o'clock at night and I was already tired. When you snooze, you lose. I should have done this before, during the day.

I unplugged the cord and pulled out the old pump and unpackaged the new one. I then slid the new PVC pipe into the new pump and placed it in the sump pump hole in order to mark the length required. This time around I decided to install a backwater valve as well. There had not been one there before, and it is a great little invention that stops water from draining back into the sump pump hole. Once the water is pumped out, it stays out. After I made the correct measurement to also include the addition of the backwater valve, I removed the new pump from the hole, pulled out the PVC pipe, and with my hacksaw cut it to the required length. I then smothered the end of it with all-purpose cement and slid it back into the base of the sump pump. It needed about a half hour to dry, so in the meantime, I began attaching one end of the backwater valve to the end of the main PVC pipe that shot the water out of the house. The little device slid over the main pipe and was secured by tightening two metal clamps. The same would happen at the other end once I placed the new sump pump into the hole.

The glue was now sufficiently dry, so I dropped the new pump into place, lined up the exposed end with the exposed end of the backwater value, and slid it in. I stepped back to make sure the PVC pipe was as straight as possible. I then plugged in the pump and hit the test button to make sure the thing was working. It came on and ran for about four seconds. That was more than enough to convince me that we were now ready for any storm. Let it rain, baby!

The next day did not disappoint. It rained elephants and rhinos. I smiled as I heard the soft purr of the sump pump. It was doing its job. I decided to go down and look at my handiwork and basically pat myself on the back. As I turned the corner to where the pump was located, I could see water on the floor. I stopped and took a deep breath. Another few steps and all I could see was water shooting sky-high out of the PVC pipe. I felt my blood pressure soaring. It looked like a garden fountain spurting water in every direction.

Very tragically, quite close to the sump pump hole was our fifty-five-inch TV and, directly below it on the TV stand, my son's video games and consoles. He loved to just plunk himself into his gaming chair and go to town, challenging all his buddies. He was a collector of video game consoles: SEGA, PlayStation, Xbox, you name it—he had just about every one ever made. It had taken him years to amass this collection. He used this corner of the basement as his man-cave gaming room. It broke my heart as I watched gallon after gallon of water cascade off the TV and onto those consoles. Everything was irreparably soaked. This was his personal hangout, and I had just destroyed it.

I sprinted over, unplugged the pump, and looked for the source of the leak. It didn't take me long to notice that I hadn't tightened down the two clamps at the lower end of the backwater value. I had just slipped the PVC pipe into it and left. When the pump came on it, the force of the water blew the pipes apart, creating a geyser. If I hadn't rushed to change the pump that night, when I was tired, and had waited until morning, I'd like to think that I would never have made such a careless mistake. Worse than that, a professional could have installed it in less than an hour. Anything they would have charged would have been worth it compared to the devastation and heartbreak I now had to impart on my son.

Fearful and afraid, I went upstairs to tell my son what had happened. His sadness and disappointment were evident, but he took it like a man. I told him I'd pay to replace the destroyed items, knowing I'd be tossing out unlimited amounts of cash, but I had to show him that his dad had some class.

**Estimated cost of job: $275**

**Actual cost of job: Ongoing**

*Episode 45*

## WEEDING OUT THE BAD FROM THE GOOD

As you probably know by now, trees and I don't see eye to eye. I've had my fair share of life-threatening run-ins, thanks very much, and wasn't eager to try my hand as an arborist again any time soon. I was now faced with a similar sort of tree situation. Our new place was blessed with a small backyard that was totally enclosed with twenty-foot cedar trees. They provided a great setting and, of course, privacy. The trees spanned across the back of the yard and down one side of the house. Stuck right in the middle of the cedars on the side was a gigantic green weed tree with an eight-inch-diameter trunk. It rose up about fifteen feet above the cedars and was a real eyesore. It couldn't be ignored. Every time I stepped onto the back deck, it was the first thing I saw. I had a tree cutting service look at it. But even with the ghosts of trees past haunting me, I wasn't about to pay the $350 they wanted to take it down. I mean, I had the necessary tools. And surely I'd learned from my past mistakes. I'd level this baby myself.

Out came my eight-foot stepladder, chain saw, reciprocating saw, extension cords, safety glasses, and gloves. The first thing I did was to go to the top of the ladder, then reach up as high as I could and attach a rope to the tree. My plan was to cut through a portion of the base of the trunk so that it would lean, pull the weed toward me with the rope, and as it slowly emerged from between the cedars, climb the ladder again to systematically chop off limbs. I would then finally cut the trunk itself into small pieces. This was the plan as the weed was far too tall and heavy to just let it fall to the ground. It was to be a gentle, controlled slice-and-dice operation. My wife had heard all the clatter and came out to see what I was doing this time. I explained my flawless plan to her and waited for her nod of approval. Instead I got her trademark "Do you think this is a good idea?" It made me pause and think for a second, and then I carried on.

Back about fifteen feet from the tree I stood on the grass, rope in hand, and started pulling with all my might. Very painfully and slowly part of the weed started to show its head, and bit by bit more of it was out and away from the cedars. I was making progress. I had to take several breaks during this tug-of-war as it was very tiring work. I got back at it with renewed energy and gave the rope a super-huge yank. Without warning, the weed, like a charging rhino, quickly started to topple right at me. I jumped out of the way as it sideswiped our umbrella, took out our wicker couch, and came to a final stop on top of the central air unit. The couch had splinters flying in all directions and a deep crater in the top of it. I was more concerned about the central air unit. I rushed over and saw that the weed had pushed in the top of the unit and twisted the fan blade and who knows what else. Who would have ever thought that this weed would have gone into a free-fall mode? I was thankful, though, as if it had taken a quick turn to the right it probably would have taken out part of the roof and gutter. Still, the overall damage was substantial. Bewildered and depressed, I grabbed my chain saw and hacked the thing into pieces.

The couch was part of a complete lawn furniture set, so I had to special order the destroyed piece. As we all know, ordering individual pieces of a set is a lot more expensive than ordering them as part of an entire set. I felt I had been gouged. As for the central air unit, the guy who came to appraise it slowly removed body parts to see the extent of the injury. He had about six bent and twisted pieces out already and was still elbow-deep in the unit, investigating. He said there was good news and bad news. The good news was that the casing for the unit could be pounded out and still used. The bad news was that the tree had pushed the blades down into the motor itself, which could not be repaired. However, a refurbished motor could be purchased at a greatly reduced price.

The cost of the repairs induced pain but not even close to the pain I experienced when I told my wife the bad news (she was less impressed with the good news). She had her doubts from the beginning about me taking on this task. It was a sixth sense—she always seemed to know when I should walk away from a job, but I never did. I recalled what she had said, and yes dear, "It wasn't a good idea."

**Estimated cost of job:** $0

**Actual cost of job:** $900

*Episode 46*

It was time to change the oil in my Ford truck. Like a trained seal I was programmed to take it into a quick one-stop lube place, wait twenty minutes, pay an arm and a leg, and then leave. I was tired of doing that. I'd seen my dad and granddad change oil over the years. They always felt a sense of satisfaction in doing it. For them, it was a given that you did your own oil changes. I thought of myself as "old-school" and was used to doing just about everything myself anyway, so why not change my own oil for the first time? Maybe it wasn't for everyone, but it was for me. I had never even stuck my head under the truck to see what was going on, but things were going to change. I'd change the oil myself and save a few bucks. I'd just mimic what my dad had done.

I decided to do it in the driveway where there was lots of room to move around. I'd have to crawl under the truck to change the oil filter. I borrowed some older, well-made drive-on ramps and carefully drove the car onto them while my wife, the spotter, guided me. I'd learned from working on my motorcycle that safety was of the utmost importance. My wife was a basket case guiding me on and was terrified that she'd guide me off, but that part went well. Before crawling under I made sure I had the necessary tools, including my hardly used work overalls, latex gloves, and my newly bought filter wrench and oil drain pan. I already had a socket set. I, of course, purchased the correct oil and oil filter from the dealership. They reminded me to change the drain plug gasket and not reuse the old one, as once disturbed it could be unreliable. Doing a quick inventory, I noticed that I'd forgotten to pick up a protective sheet to put under the car. It was on my list, but I wasn't going back to the store. I'd just have to be extra careful.

As always, I had some tunes playing in the background. Country music was my go-to. I particularly liked the station that played the slow and easy hits. It was always laid-back and not too intense. You could do your work and it would soothe your soul all at once. Some of the new music these days would have me grinding my teeth.

I could tell I was getting older as lying on the interlocking bricks was very uncomfortable. I eyeballed the oil pan to make sure the old oil coming out would drain as close to the center of the pan as possible. I got the right size socket and removed the drain plug quickly to avoid oil spraying outside of the pan. I then wrenched off the old oil filter and made sure that none of the seal had stuck to the engine. I installed the new filter and tightened both it and the drain plug. I reexamined my steps to make sure I hadn't missed anything and crawled from under the car feeling confident that everything was bang-on. I poured in the new oil, let the car run for a while, and then crawled back under to make sure there were no leaks. I knew there wouldn't be any. I backed the car off the ramps, let the oil settle, topped it up a bit, and then did one final dipstick reading. Everything was perfect. I shut the hood and went in the house to celebrate with a beer.

About an hour or so later, I had to run an errand. I jumped in the car and backed it out of the driveway. As I turned my head to go forward, I notice a huge black spot in the middle of my driveway. I jumped out and soon realized that it was oil— and about a two-foot circle of it. What an eyesore. A black hole in the middle of our beautiful interlocking brick driveway. I was sick. I couldn't imagine how this had happened as I was extremely careful in changing the oil. I slipped my hands into my pockets as I stared at this mess and felt something there. I pulled out the new drain plug gasket. I had shoved it in my pocket as I crawled under the car and had obviously forgotten to change it. I went to the car, stuck my melon under it, and could see oil steadily dripping from the drain plug. I was ready to toss my cookies. The source of the problem was discovered, and it was me. There was nothing I could do now, so I drove to the quick lube place around the corner, had him drain the oil, put in new oil, and correctly replace the drain plug. Once again, I was stiffed with a bill.

I was afraid to go straight home, so I went to the closest hardware store and picked up some guaranteed-to-work oil remover and a large broom. I parked quietly at the front of the house and snuck up to the oil slick and started working. By the time I finished the oil was now three feet in diameter and looked worse than ever. This stuff was useless. I had failed and was now going to have to face the music. I called my wife out. The tongue lashing wasn't as bad as some in the past.

I had no choice but to call the brick people in the hope that they had some miraculous formula for cleaning up the oil. After a quick inspection the guy said there was no way on earth that the oil was going to come off the bricks. The oil had soaked into them, and they could not be reclaimed. I'd have to rip them up and replace them. He said it was a time-consuming job, as the stained bricks had to be pried out, new special sand put down, then tapped down and leveled, followed by new bricks being carefully positioned into place. He didn't volunteer the cost and I didn't ask. An oil change was supposed to be so easy that even a twelve-year-old kid could probably do it, yet I managed to mess it up. It really only involves about five steps. My first step should have been to leave the damn thing alone.

**Estimated cost of job:** $55

**Actual cost of job:** $780 (including driveway repair)

## *Episode 47*

## WHAT A DRIP!

**W**e'd had this dripping tap in our bathroom for a long time. I'd been able to ignore it, but two years in, every time I saw it, it drove me crazy. I tried turning the cold tap on and off numerous times to see if it was just a fluke thing, but the drip didn't go away. I was sure it was just an old, worn-out cartridge that was causing the problem and really not that difficult to replace. The switch in the cartridge is supposed to block off or open the hot and cold water lines, but it clearly was not doing its job anymore. A plumber was out of the question. With what they charged, I'd only call on them if it was an emergency and this was not. I could handle this job.

I was shocked that the new cartridge I picked up at the local hardware store was free. I asked the sales guy if he had made a mistake. I couldn't ever remember anything being free. He said that some plumbing manufacturers offered free plastic cartridge replacements. The original cartridges were usually metal, but once they wore out one could pick up plastic replacements whenever needed, at no charge. Of course, the purchaser would have to do the installation. Once home, I turned the water off under the sink and then proceeded to take the tap apart. All I had to do was take out the top screw holding the handle in place, remove the gold horseshoe bracket holding the cartridge in place, and finally, with an adjustable wrench or pair of pliers, pull out the old cartridge. A five-minute job, tops! In seconds I was down to pulling out the old cartridge. I tried twisting it back and forth to loosen it, but it wouldn't budge. It had been in there for years and was clearly stuck. With the new cartridge came a white plastic cap that was designed to fit over the old cartridge. One could then place the wrench around the cap and simply twist it until the cartridge became unstuck. It was a good plan, only it didn't work. The damn thing had a mind of its own and wouldn't move even a smidgen. I didn't want to force anything and make it worse, so I went online to check out the next best step. Up popped another gadget, better than the white cap, so off I went to the hardware store and purchased it for a mere $30. It was guaranteed never to fail. I followed the same procedure as before with the same result. That cartridge simply would not waver. It seemed to be cemented in there. Back I went to the video again for plan C. It outlined a kind of last-resort move whereby you built a makeshift contraption that allowed you to apply leverage and pry it straight up and out. This was intended for the truly desperate, but it made sense to me. And at this point it was a Hail Mary or give up and call the plumber.

So I dug up two two-by-fours, each roughly five inches long, and grabbed some large vice grips. As shown, I placed the first piece of wood flat on the surface to the right of the tap, two inches in from the right side of the sink top. The second piece of wood was turned on its side and placed on top of the first piece of wood, close to the tap. The plan was to then place the grips on top of the wood, tightly lock them on the top of the cartridge, and simply push down on the handle end of the grips. It would act like a seesaw, and the leverage should pop the cartridge out. Ingenious really! If this wasn't enough, I could then use the original wrench for additional leverage. I pushed down hard on the grips handle, and to my disappointment the cartridge still didn't budge at all. I got the other wrench, put it sideways on top of the wood, and started again. I now had about another three inches of leverage which should do the trick. I grunted, groaned, and cursed as I tried to get that thing out, but again no luck. I assumed at this point that more brute force was required, so I put both hands on the end of the wrench, basically lifted myself right off the ground, and gave it everything I had. The cartridge started to rise just as the corner of the porcelain sink cracked and crashed to the ground. I broke into a sweat staring at the grapefruit-size chunk of porcelain lying in pieces on the floor and tried to think of some solution to this disaster. If it was just one slab, I might have been able to glue it back on, but in pieces, there was no hope.

The only thing to do now was pack up my tools and tell my wife the bad news.

Unfortunately for me, this particular bathroom sink was a colonial style. The classic white basin was mounted on an elegant stand, all carved from one piece. It wasn't one of the cheaper models out there. And as it had to match the other bathroom fixtures and because our other bathroom was colonial in style as well, I had no choice but to track down a similar sink. It was, of course, a special order. It had to come from a certain high-end manufacturer. I cringed as the sales associate read out the price, but I was stuck. I had the option to pick it up myself and avoid the three-week wait, but I declined, thinking of my past road trips.

Estimated cost of repairs: $0

Actual cost of repairs: $365

*Episode 48*

A neighbor of mine was kind enough to give me a shelving unit that was just lying in pieces in her garage, collecting dust. No matter how hard I tried, I always had junk lying around on the garage floor. There were extension cords, a leaf blower, rags, oil, work gloves, recyclable bins, and a multitude of other things as well. Too many to even mention. In addition to wanting to get them in some kind of organized fashion, it was just a matter of time before I tripped over something and twisted an ankle or cut open my noggin. It would be perfect for my garage. I brought over the pieces and put it together on my garage floor. It was a really nice unit, with a strong frame, metal shelves, and even bracketing on the back part of the frame to attach it to the garage wall. It was a beauty when assembled: ten feet high, four feet wide, with seven shelves.

When I stood it up and pushed it into its new home, touching the back wall and one side wall, it looked like a million bucks. As a precautionary measure, I always felt it wise to secure shelves like this to the back wall. I had a mishmash of screws, bolts, nuts, washers, and many other things in my basement that I could use to secure it in place. The screws I found would do the job, but I would have preferred them to be a little longer. Normally I used hollow metal anchors to attach a unit like this to the drywall at the back of the garage. Making a small hole in the drywall, these anchors could be tapped into place with a hammer. This type of anchor, once put into the drywall, would expand and grip as the screw was tightened into it and would be almost impossible to get back out. I didn't have any of them, so I used some basic plastic ones I had lying around instead. These worked similarly but did not grip much at all. I was so excited to finish mounting the unit that I didn't want to waste time going to the hardware store. Besides, why throw away hard-earned money when I already had something that would probably work?

I drilled holes in the bracketing at the back of the unit, hammered in the plastic anchors, and tightened the screws. To be overly cautious, I put anchors and screws on each side of the top four shelves. The last thing I'd want would be for the unit to fall over and land on my little sports car! Confident that the unit was not going anywhere, I stacked all kinds of tools and other junk on the shelves. I was so pleased at how many things I was able to get off the garage floor and into the unit.

A week or so later it was time to trim the cedar trees that lined the side of the house. I grabbed my hedge trimmer and headed to the garage to fetch my extension cord. I always stored it quite high up on the shelving unit since I didn't use it that often and so kept it out of the way. I reached up as high as I could, grabbed part of the cord, and pulled on it. It unraveled as I walked out of the garage. I didn't get fifteen feet before I heard a creaking. I turned around and saw the entire unit pulling away from the back wall, tilting ominously and ever so slowly forward. I hadn't paid attention when pulling on the extension cord. It had gotten snagged on the front end of the shelf and became wedged in there. I was literally tugging on the entire unit. My first thought was to run back and try to keep the unit from falling, Hercules style, but with so much stuff on it, it was way too heavy. Instead, I was forced to watch it tumble over like a slow-moving turtle. On its way down, it grabbed my bicycle and then the kids' bicycles, all of which were hanging from hooks on the side wall of the garage. As it progressed down, it clutched a shelf I had installed at the bottom of the window. I wasn't too upset about the shelf, but I was extremely upset about my cell phone and Bluetooth speaker, both of which I had set there for safekeeping. With a loud bang and a puff of dust, the unit crashed on the floor with three bikes, a speaker, and cell phone thoroughly flattened under it. I could only be thankful that my car wasn't in the garage at the time.

I knew right away what had happened. I was truly upset and kicked myself a few times. The screws and anchors I had used pulled right out of the back wall with ease when I started yanking on the jammed extension cord. If I'd put my ass in gear and driven to the hardware store a few minutes away

B.S. Harris

to buy the right anchors and screws, I wouldn't have experienced this costly disaster. I was a disgrace again and replacing the destroyed items would be breathtaking.

Estimated cost: $0

Actual cost: $1,600

*Episode 49*

## THE MAKING OF MEMORIES

I was in a mellow mood one night. I was by myself, sitting outside, staring into the darkness, and sipping on a drink. I thought about many things in my life and somehow started reminiscing about the house we had left a few years before. We had lived there thirty years. Our kids were born and raised there. It had been a great house and held great memories. It was an old house when we first moved in and needed repair work done from day one. I laughed as I recalled some of my work projects. They weren't funny at the time, but they were now.

The new people hadn't been in the house even a day when they called the real estate agent, who in turn called me. The people said that there was no hot water in the upstairs shower. I told the agent that the tap was reversed. Turn it to the hot side and cold water comes out and vice versa. When I was replacing a defective cartridge, I mistakenly put the new one in upside down and then couldn't get it out again, so we lived with it. Once you knew what to do, life was good.

A few days later the same agent called me again. I had

installed a ceiling light in the front entrance, but the owners couldn't find the light switch. I explained that the switch was down the hall and in the closet, hidden behind the door. I remember that particular project. I was unable to run the electrical wire for the light anywhere near it, so I ended up finding the first available spot which was about twenty feet down the hall and in the closet. Sometimes the best-made plans don't work.

I smiled as I thought back over the years in that house. There were so many projects. Did any of them ever go to plan? I recalled fondly the time there was a leak behind the shower head in the downstairs bathroom. I had taken off the shower head and could see the leaking pipe directly behind it. It was going to be a hell of a job to fix this, as I would have to rip out a bunch of tiles just to get at it. A huge job I was just not interested in tackling. So I did what any prudent handyman would do: I reached into the existing hole and tightly wrapped duct tape around the pipe and then forgot it even existed. When we left the house, it was only leaking a little.

Then there was the time I rebuilt the back deck. It must have been one hundred degrees outside that day. It was a great weight-loss program working out there, as I must have sweated off ten pounds. I was drained by the time I had ripped off all the old, rotted deck boards. I had torn out the old framework under the boards and was starting from scratch. As I started building the new framework, I realized partway through that I had not bought enough of the metal corner brackets that joined the wood together. I was way too hot and unmotivated at that point to make another trip to the hardware store, so I simply used the brackets on every other juncture. I didn't realize until I put the new deck boards down that there was quite a sway when you walked around. The family knew the soft areas, so they could navigate the terrain. I'm sure the new owners would catch on in short order.

And, of course, I never forgot the time a guest of ours was having a smoke on our front porch and accidentally set the wooden steps on fire. We put the fire out quickly, but the stairs were now charred and black. It would take great effort to remove and replace the four damaged steps, as they were very old and solidly hammered in. Instead I grabbed some very rough grit sandpaper and scrapped off as much of the black as I could. I then slopped on as much stain as possible and hoped the stairs sort of matched the undamaged stairs. Not my best work, but I didn't get a call from the agent.

Whenever anyone slammed the front door, pieces of stucco would fall from the ceiling. Once I had a collection of these pieces, I felt it was time to try to put them back where they came from, if I could find the correct spots. To re-stucco a ceiling was a huge and messy job. If it was a small piece, I used Krazy Glue. If it was a larger piece, I used duct tape. I would stick it on the back of the stucco and then fold the tape backward and ram it into the hole and hope that the piece stayed there. It usually did. If one didn't stare too intently at the ceiling, one would never know.

B.S. Harris

Memories kept coming back to me, but before too long the siren of my to-do list dragged me back to the present. In our new place my toolbox was just inside our front door. And no doubt there would be many more memories to make soon enough.

**Estimated cost of memories:** $71,785

**Actual cost of memories:** Priceless

*Conclusion*

**B**eing a handy person is something everyone should attempt at some point in their lives. We all need to challenge ourselves from time to time. It can be a confidence booster at times and downright disappointing at others, but it's always good to step out of your comfort zone and take a chance once in a while. Never take on something too involved in the beginning. Work your way up. You will be pleasantly surprised when you learn a few "tricks of the trade." As the old saying goes: "Nothing ventured, nothing gained!" And remember, it's okay to laugh at your mistakes—everyone else will.

Becoming a handyman has taught me a lot, which can be nicely summed up in this phrase: "I wish I knew then what I know now." On the other hand, if I did know then what I know now, I probably wouldn't have attempted to fix half of the things I've tried to fix over the years . . . and I would never have come to the place where I know things that I didn't know then. Clear as mud, right?

Be aware that once the world knows that you are handy, there will be challenges and sacrifices:

1. Your home to-do list will now be longer than ever

2. Your neighbors and friends will seem a lot friendlier

3. You will start talking to yourself much more

4. Black and blue will become permanent colors for your thumb

5. Your bank account will often be drained from having the pros fix your mistakes

6. Stress levels in the household will sky-rocket

7. Self-confidence will be shaky at best

8. You will miss watching many hockey games

9. Your vehicle will have a lot more mileage on it thanks to those countless trips to the hardware store

10. You will create multiple opportunities to amuse your friends and family

As I said in the beginning of the book, we all have a lit-tle cheap handyman or -woman in us, whether we choose to admit it or not. So, get out there and have some fun!

Oh, and one last piece of advice? If you do not complete the job successfully: Silence! If you do complete the job suc-cessfully: Tell everyone you know and everyone you don't know that you nailed it!

## ACKNOWLEDGMENTS

I would like to thank my US editor, Hannah Robinson, for her tireless assistance in bringing *The Cheap Handyman* to fruition. Hannah spent countless hours making this book the best it could be. Her attention to detail, her sense of humor, and sound ideas brought the book to a higher level. And thank you also to my Canadian editor, Justin Stoller of Simon & Schuster Canada. Through our talks I always found Justin willing and ready to discuss any aspects of the book. His creative ideas and suggestions made for welcome additions to *The Cheap Handyman* and enhanced it. It has been a memorable journey.

I'd also like to thank the team at Tiller Press for their contributions, especially Laura Flavin, Molly Pieper, Kayla Bartee, Lauren Ollerhead, Michael Andersen, Annie Craig, Laura Levatino, Jonathan Evans, and Theresa DiMasi for their dedicated help. Extra big thanks also to Patrick Sullivan for coming up with such a cool cover. And at Simon & Schuster Canada, Mackenzie Croft, Laura MacDonald, and Paul Barker all helped bring the book to the world.

I want to extend my eternal gratitude to my literary agent,

## Acknowledgments

Lloyd Kelly of Kelly Consulting Agency, without whose assistance, support, and encouragement this book may never have gone to print. He was able to see the big picture, and his guidance and wisdom brought *The Cheap Handyman* to where it is now. It has truly been a pleasure working with him, and I look forward to the day when we can work together again.

**B.S. Harris** is happily retired, which provides him with even more time to hang out in hardware stores and, of course, tinker and repair just about anything that breaks down around his family dwelling. He grew up in an average, hardworking home and was fortunate enough to earn a post-secondary degree. He is an amateur athlete and musician, and a lifelong motorcycle enthusiast. He and his very understanding family live in Southern Ontario, Canada.